Our Way

Family, Parish, and Neighborhood
in a Polish-American Community

Our Way

Family, Parish, and Neighborhood
in a Polish-American Community

PAUL WROBEL

UNIVERSITY OF NOTRE DAME PRESS
NOTRE DAME ~ LONDON

0 9 8 7 6 5 4 3 2 1

Library of Congress Cataloging in Publication Data

Wrobel, Paul, 1942–
    Our way.

    Includes bibliographical references and index.
    1. Polish Americans—Michigan—Detroit—Social
conditions. 2. Catholics—Michigan—Detroit—Social
conditions. 3. Detroit—Social conditions. I. Title.
F574.D49P78   301.45′19′185077434   78-62967
ISBN 0-268-01494-9

Manufactured in the United States of America

For

Kathleen

Contents

Acknowledgments

This book is a revised and expanded version of a doctoral dissertation I completed in 1975 for the Anthropology Department of Catholic University of America. My graduate studies there were completed under a traineeship from the National Science Foundation, while fieldwork in Detroit as well as the writing-up phase were supported by grants from the Rockefeller Foundation, the National Institute of Mental Health, and the Kosciuszko Foundation. I am grateful to those organizations for their financial assistance.

I wish to thank the members of my doctoral committee at Catholic University for their guidance and encouragement. Professor Lucy Cohen, my chairperson, taught me a great deal through asking relevant questions instead of telling me what to do, and Professors Regina F. Herzfeld and Phyllis P. Chock were demanding readers with a concern for both content and style.

Many people from the Detroit area were also helpful. While it is impossible to mention everyone who assisted me in my work, I would like to express my appreciation to Professors Otto Feinstein, John Gutowski, and Bryan Thompson, all of Wayne State University.

Professor Thaddeus C. Radzialowski, of Minnesota's Southwest State University, and Mrs. Regina Koscielska, of Hamtramck, Michigan, were kind enough to read the original dissertation and provide detailed comments which influenced the revisions I made in the present work.

I owe a special debt of gratitude to Dr. Stephen Emelock, whose editorial advice was of vital importance in my attempt to make the stylistic changes which distinguish a dissertation from a readable book.

My dedicated and loyal secretary at the Merrill-Palmer Institute, Mrs. Irene Zakrzewski, demonstrated particular competence, both in typing early drafts of the revised manuscript and in handling public reaction to the media's interpretation of my research findings. Mrs. Helen Maturi typed the final manuscript with great care and patience.

I also wish to thank the pastor and parishioners of St. Thaddeus for allowing me and my family to become a part of their community, thus making this study possible.

Finally, I will always be grateful to Kathleen Rogers Wrobel. For being herself.

Foreword

I have always had problems reading books written by social scientists about experiences that I had lived and shared. The books seemed far too complicated and the scholarship too burdensome to reveal anything appealing about the subject matter. Paul Wrobel represents a new breed of social scientists, or at least I hope this book becomes a model for a new style of presenting the data that has been laboriously and painstakingly wrung from the subject under study. Paul Wrobel's book puts the reader directly in touch with the values, mores, and social patterns of one Detroit Polish-American community. Having read his book, I feel I know the community well, not just its face, but its heart and soul.

Wrobel's success has to do with his own erudition, but also his method. He doesn't write as a detached observer. Lord, save us from that kind of social scientist! They end up knowing as much about the social groups they study as someone studying the mating habits of tropical fish by observing the ten-gallon tank on top of a television set. Paul Wrobel writes as a participant observer. He lived in and with the community he talks about. He experienced their pains, their joys, their successes. And so did his wife and children. He didn't just find out what the social patterns were, but he became emmeshed in them.

Only with this kind of approach could one ever understand my mother's comment to my brother and me one Thanksgiving. We were in a heated debate over the rights of Blacks in American society. Momma came into the room and said: "Stop your arguing. We're all Americans. It's Thanksgiving. Eat your spaghetti."

Wrobel's study is of an American ethnic group. Some fellow anthropologists will probably give it disapproving nods. After all, ethnic groups are disappearing faster than the American eagle. If they aren't, they probably should, in the opinion of most social scientists. Wrobel, they might add, should be about more important things.

Like what? I would venture to ask. Ethnic group interaction is one of the primary, enduring, and most important ways Americans relate to each other. How are we going to become more American unless we go about trying to understand our differences as well as our commonalities? We know more about the Aborigines in Australia than we do about the Poles in Detroit. My nephew Rodney knows more about American Eskimos than about the Blacks in Philadelphia. Yet he has to share the same slice of American Pie with those Blacks. How much better off would he be if he understood the values, needs, mores, and social patterns of the people whom he would encounter each day of his life?

Wrobel's book is one fine step for the Poles of Detroit and one giant step for the American people. We need more studies like this, and perhaps fewer rockets.

And you don't have to be Polish to enjoy it. While there are many differences between the Polish and my Italian heritage, many of his stories stirred memories in my mind about my early life with my immigrant parents in a small coal mining town in Pennsylvania. In the story of this particular experience of a particular Polish community in Detroit, the story of everyman echoes. Paul Wrobel has done us all a service.

In a personal way, Paul Wrobel represents a new breed of American social scientists—a person of vision and spirit who served in a second culture experience with the Peace Corps in Africa and then returned to his roots and to a neighborhood similar to the one in which he grew up, to study and reflect upon a central question for all Americans: Who am I and who are we as Americans in this world that is indeed an intercultural village? The future of race relations as well as critical issues of domestic and foreign policy will be better served by the discipline of the new pluralists like Wrobel who may help us recognize that we need not "melt, or get off the pot," but rather realize, like René Dubos, that it is important and necessary to "tolerate diversity if we are to survive." Wrobel's book is part of a new reflection that will serve us all as we struggle with how better to shape and share the burden of social change—as well as face up to the reality that we are all valued variants of a common humanity.

Geno C. Baroni

Introduction

1

This book is about working-class Polish Americans who belong to the same Roman Catholic parish and reside in its surrounding neighborhood. My inquiry was not guided by a set of hypotheses, nor did I set out to compile generalizations about Polish Americans and the process of assimilation. Rather, what I have attempted to do, as an anthropologist, is to learn as much as possible about the culture and community of Polish Americans from a particular place—a neighborhood in Detroit, Michigan—at a particular time—the early 1970s.[1]

My plans to embark on this project began to take shape when a colleague asked me, "Is it true that you speak an African language but have never been able to converse with your own grandmother?" Ironically, it *was* true. I could manage a few words in Polish, including various greetings and names of certain foods, and with some assistance I could even count to ten. But like many third-generation Polish Americans I found it impossible to carry on a conversation with a grandparent who spoke only Polish. Indeed, I felt much more comfortable speaking the African language I had learned while serving in Sierra Leone as a Peace Corps Volunteer. My friend thought this was hilarious, but I found myself thinking that here was a perfect example of how assimilation worked in American society. Yet language isn't everything, I mused on; what about day-to-day life in an ethnic community? Are there distinct cultural differences among the many ethnic groups in our country? Or does the image of a melting pot accurately depict American society? I didn't know, and, until recently, I didn't really care. But now I was curious.

I became even more interested in those questions as a result of

1

participating in a conference on ethnic community development sponsored by Catholic University and the Task Force on Urban Problems from the United States Catholic Conference. Its goal, in the words of Msgr. Geno Baroni, the director, was "to help the white ethnic groups develop the organizational skills and structure prerequisite to solving the social and economic problems which beset their communities."[2]

Community leaders from all over the nation attended, as well as social scientists and political figures. At the heart of the conference was a series of small group meetings during which participants discussed the unmet needs of urban ethnic working-class people and their communities. I acted as a recorder at many of those meetings, and in the course of lengthy and sometimes heated discussions I heard Polish Americans, Italian Americans, and others decry their lack of economic resources. I heard them speak passionately of their estrangement from government, their alienation from the larger society. I heard their problems, a whole host of them, from care for the aged to the destruction of ethnic neighborhoods.

Yet, above all, I could hear people speak proudly if not nostalgically of their ethnic background, arguing that America was not a melting pot, that ethnicity was still important in American life. Gradually I became convinced that my own ethnic group was as fascinating a subject for study as any I could find. So my plans to return to Africa were put aside; I would live and work in an urban Polish-American neighborhood instead of a rural African village.

Detroit was the logical setting. I had already established contact with the pastor of a Polish parish there who had shown an interest in my work and suggested his neighborhood as a place to live. Furthermore, I was interested in keeping close tabs on the recently formed Black/Polish Conference, a Detroit-based alliance of Blacks and Poles whose objective was

> to promote each group's independence and separate cultural values while, at the same time, promoting maximum cooperation and understanding between the two largest ethnic groups in the greater Detroit area.[3]

But soon after my arrival I learned that the Black/Polish Conference found it impossible to mobilize support and create an effective organizational base.

I also became aware of the significance of the parish in the lives of my new Polish-American neighbors. The weekly schedule in the church paper listed an event, and often two or three, almost every evening. There were meetings of numerous parish societies, gatherings of boy scouts, girl scouts, senior citizens, and the teen club. The list also included weekly bingo as well as a liturgy meeting. Also, parishioners could attend mass and have their confessions heard in Polish. While I was acquainted with many Catholic parishes throughout the nation, I had never seen one so alive, so vibrant. Every church provides for the religious needs of its parishioners, but this one obviously played a very important role in fulfilling their social requirements as well.

I knew William Thomas and Florian Znaniecki had emphasized the importance of the parish in the lives of Polish Americans, but their research was conducted more than fifty years ago.[4] Furthermore, other more recent studies on assimilation and the parish had led me to expect that if the parish existed at all, its role in the community would no longer be important.[5] Clearly, in this instance, that was not the case.

The fact that the parish was still thriving, that it was the center of social and religious life for the American Poles in my new neighborhood was indeed strong evidence of the continuing importance of ethnicity on the contemporary scene in the United States. It would be of interest, I thought, to focus my study on the parish and its members. For in addition to providing a glimpse of what life is like in an urban ethnic community, perhaps I could demonstrate that assimilation had not taken place as quickly as many writers would have us believe.

Yet studying a Polish parish through the traditional anthropological approach of participant observation, a methodology I was firmly committed to, presented a serious problem. For my wife and I had already faced difficulties in finding a home, making friends, and being accepted into the community.

FINDING A HOME

It took over two months to find a suitable place for our family, which included two young children under three. During that period I daily combed the city and local newspapers to no avail. Houses were not for rent, and the available upper flats excluded children. I then placed ads in four newspapers, including the parish weekly, and the *Dziennik Polski*, which published in Polish. I specified that we wanted a house in the parish area and that we would remain for at least two years. We received several calls, but none of the properties was in the required vicinity.

Next I walked around the neighborhood to talk to people and inquire about places for rent, and I visited every bar and restaurant, hoping to touch base with someone who could help. Still no luck. What's more, I had encountered a deluge of hostility, even reluctance to converse on the weather. My dress made no difference. Whether I wore a sportcoat and tie or not, most of the people, either watering their lawns or sitting on their porches, wouldn't deign to so much as look up in response to my greetings or inquiries. Many refused to speak. Some either ignored me or answered with a nod. As frustrating as it was, I knew those first encounters were telling me something about the nature of life in this community—anthropologically, that is. Nevertheless, it wasn't until much later that I understood the reasons behind their reactions.

Finally, I took my family on a walking tour of the neighborhood and elicited a completely opposite response. People were willing to engage in conversation, going out of their way to be helpful. At one point we were offered three flats within the same block; a woman with whom we were talking waved to two other women and asked them to join our discussion. Apparently they were neighbors. And before we knew it, all of us were inspecting upper flats, with each neighbor, in turn, commenting on the cleanliness and desirability of the other's home. Unfortunately, none of those flats was large enough for a family of four. Then, soon after, we spotted an ad in a local paper and rented a house that seemed to suit our needs, only to learn later that it did not measure up to tacitly understood standards set by people of the community.[6]

Also, I discovered why it had been so difficult to find a place at first, and what was responsible for the hostility I had encountered when walking through the neighborhood without my family.

There had been a series of burglaries just before my arrival, and because I was a stranger some may have suspected me of "casing the joint." In retrospect, that is not surprising: Later my wife and I had similar feelings when someone unfamiliar appeared on the block, especially after our house had been ransacked three times. We knew virtually everyone who passed our home, and usually where they were going and where they had been. So if a stranger walked by we immediately got a bit suspicious. Since that aptly describes how most of the people felt, no wonder they cold-shouldered me.

In addition to burglars, the neighbors had been harried by real estate dealers, both Black and white, who attempted to coerce them into selling their homes, suggesting that Blacks were moving in en masse. I had been mistaken for a real estate dealer. Some people subsequently told me they were convinced of this when I had inquired into rentals; they had seen my approach as a foot-in-the-door ploy to make a deal.

When I brought my family all that changed, of course; they saw husband and father rather than burglar or real estate huckster.

Still, there remains one more obstacle facing strangers seeking housing in this community; many of the flats and houses rent by word of mouth, not newspaper ads. When a place becomes available, word travels quickly via Metropolitan Detroit's Polish-American communication network. And herein a twofold purpose is served: first, the rental gets to be "advertised"; and second, the prospective tenant is evaluated either "good" or "bad" by members of the "closed-circuit hook-up." Since we were not as privy to such a network it was difficult to hear of what was available and, in turn, as difficult for landlords to determine whether we were desirable. All considered, then, we were fortunate to have found a house.

MAKING FRIENDS AND ESTABLISHING AN ACCEPTABLE ROLE

To further complicate matters, we also found it hard getting acquainted with people and becoming accepted in the parish. I had joined the Dad's Club and my wife, the Madonna Guild, so we involved ourselves in the two most important parish organizations. That notwithstanding, we were still strangers. And, even though we attended every activity and event, including my becoming a substitute in the bowling league, we didn't really know anybody and felt we weren't learning anything. Also, I had not established myself in a role that was both acceptable and easily understood.

Seeing my car home during the day, neighbors would ask my wife if I worked either the afternoon or midnight shift. When told I was a student studying the history of the parish and neighborhood, their brows would furrow even more quizzically. It was difficult for them to grasp how a thirty-year-old married man with two children could still be a student. Besides, albeit they could hear me pounding away on my electric typewriter, they felt something was wrong because I didn't "work." Sitting behind a desk at home wasn't their idea of employment, and it was a stigma to be jobless. I was therefore a curious figure and that concerned me; without an acceptable and easily understood role it would be impossible to conduct a successful study.

However, the major obstacles to becoming a participant observer were the social and cultural characteristics of this community. There are no street-corner men here, nor do people gather regularly in their respective homes, as Gans describes for the Italians in Boston.[7] As one informant put it, "People like to keep to themselves behind closed doors." For example, it is not uncommon for neighbors to live next to each other for thirty-five years without either ever having entered the other's house. In short, the home is of little importance as a gathering place.

That function is fulfilled by the parish, with its numerous activities. But they were held mainly in the evening; and although we were involved, we were not getting a chance to observe the whole round of life, from child-rearing to table manners. Moreover, we noticed that people were very cautious in establishing relationships with newcomers, even a fellow Polish American. Thus it was becoming increasingly clear that my revised plans would also have to be shelved if the situation continued much longer.

Luckily for me, a teacher in the parish grade school left in mid-year, and the pastor asked if I would take a job. I was delighted to, for it seemed like an excellent chance to establish an acceptable role and proceed with my study. So for six months I became a teacher of seventh- and eighth-grade English, reading, and music. Teaching school was a difficult experience, but it gave me an entrée into the community, and enabled me to gain insights into its social and cultural characteristics, especially family life.

Before accepting the job I explained my purposes to the pastor and the school's principal. They needed a teacher, and I agreed to fulfill that position diligently; nevertheless I wanted it clearly understood that I saw this as an opportunity to act as a participant observer. They agreed and it presented few problems, at least as far as I was concerned. I took daily notes on events in class and in the faculty room, and on the inevitable contacts a teacher has with parents.

In addition to my own observations, the children were asked, as part of their English assignments, to write compositions on their neighborhood. And later I initiated an essay project called "Operation Ancestors" with twenty-five students of a seventh-grade class. I had taken the idea from *Today's Catholic Teacher*, a magazine available in our faculty room, because it seemed exciting both as a lesson and as a procedure for my study. The children were asked to write a piece on their family history and cultural heritage, with an outline and adequate preparation provided by me. Both maternal and paternal ancestors were to be included. I adapted the general outline suggested in the magazine article, but also showed the children how to make kinship charts to include in their essays if they chose. The parents were informed of the project in a detailed memorandum describing the assignment and my own objectives. If there was an objection, they were asked to contact me directly or through their child. I had already prepared alternative assignments, but fortunately all agreed to cooperate. I also mentioned in the communication that I might like to interview them at a later date. But that was an afterthought, for I had not yet decided to conduct formal interviews. In all, the project turned out quite successfully, and many of the children who were reluctant at the onset later expressed pleasure in having learned of their family background and heritage. Parents were pleased too, and some thanked me for assigning what they considered an interesting and informative project.

Now I was accepted and known in the community. Soon after,

one of the women my wife knew from a parish society gave a small party to introduce her friends to the "new teacher's wife." I was invited to join the men's baseball team, and we both were asked to become members of the parish bowling league. Before long, we were almost too busy; for in addition to our social activities we were now expected to perform tasks as members of the parish societies. I helped work with the younger boys in basketball and other sports, and Kathleen, my wife, became involved on the committees of various clubs. We sold tickets for the annual parish festival, at which I was a security guard and my wife, a waitress in the casino.

Both of us took notes on everything we participated in, often sitting up nights, late, comparing and contrasting our observations. So in a sense this study was done by two anthropologists. My wife's participation in the community was intensive and meaningful. And her observations, especially on women and children, are an important contribution.

INTERVIEWS

Despite our growing involvement once my teaching had begun, I was still concerned with not learning enough. We had friends now, but rarely were we invited into people's homes. Nor did we entertain. First of all, since it wasn't customary we felt people might be uncomfortable. But secondly, and perhaps more important, we knew selecting whom to invite would present a real problem. For in such a small and tightly knit group everyone would know who was invited and the excluded might easily have hard feelings. It seemed necessary, then, to supplement our participant observation with formal interviews to fill in the gaps.

My first thought was to select a random sample from the community. But then I remembered the difficulties of building rapport and establishing trust, and decided to interview in depth the parents whose children had participated in "Operation Ancestors." I already knew most of them and they seemed to trust me. Furthermore, I felt that the results of interviews are always more meaningful when the researcher knows the difference between what his subjects say and what they do. Interviewing individuals with whom

I was familiar would probably result in a richer quality of data: people who knew and trusted me would tend to be more open and candid. While choosing a random sample made sense in theory, the realities of the field situation necessitated another tack.

The interview schedule was modeled after the one used by Bennett Berger in *Working-Class Suburb*. [8] Certain questions were designed to elicit information in areas where my knowledge was meager, while others helped to check on what I thought I already knew. Twenty interviews were conducted from February to June of 1973, and most of those were held in the evening with husband and wife present. Some questions were directed specifically at him, others, her, but the great majority at both. The results were then tabulated taking care to include independent responses, though the entire sample was too small to be of any statistical purpose.

The longest interview lasted just under six hours, and the shortest, two; the rest averaged about two-and-a-half hours. I began the first of them by asking each question as worded in the schedule. But that seemed to disrupt the flow of conversation, and I could see people getting tense, anticipating the questions and their replies. I therefore changed to incorporating the interview into an extended conversation, with all queries dovetailed into the dialogue when it seemed appropriate. Often I would accept a bottle of beer or a mixed drink, hoping to add to a congenial atmosphere. For the most part people seemed to enjoy being interviewed, and many invited me back. However, there were difficulties in setting up the interviews.

When I phoned people to request the interview and arrange an appointment, I explained that it was to follow up "Operation Ancestors." Though everybody remembered the project, most were reluctant to participate. Their most common response was, "I can't help you because I don't know very much." At first I sensed being misunderstood and explained that my purpose was not to request information on Poland or facts on the history of the parish. I even gave examples of the questions. Still their reluctance continued. I eventually discovered that people felt that someone with an advanced degree would certainly not be interested in the opinions, attitudes, and way of life of a person who worked in a factory and

had little education. Their other concern revolved around a desire
to maintain privacy. They as well as I knew the effects of gossip in
this community, and it didn't seem prudent to answer personal
questions directed at them by another member of the parish.
Those were major problems, but they were surmounted: In the
end only three people declined, and two others demurred because
of illness. So in total there were twenty interviews.[9]

In addition to participant observation and quasi-formal interviews, the following sources were used in this study: U.S. Census
data; parish records and census reports; and the R. L. Polk City
Directory. The latter was helpful in determining what percentage
of the people living in this area were members of the parish. By
comparing the list of parishioners against the directory that was
easily obtained.[10]

There are three additional points germane to how this study was
conducted that need to be discussed: (1) variations in the participant observer role; (2) methods of analyzing the data gathered; (3)
the ethical problems of doing a participant observer study.

VARIATIONS IN
THE PARTICIPANT–OBSERVER ROLE

Several social scientists have written that participant observation
is a generic term for a research method that actually entails a
variety of different approaches. But most useful for our purposes is
the classification provided by Herbert Gans, which is based on the
behavior of the researcher as he interacts with his subjects. Briefly,
Gans suggests that there are three types of participant observation:

1. Researcher acts as observer. In this approach the researcher is
    physically present at the event which he observes, but does not
    really participate in it.
2. Researcher participates, but as researcher. In this case, the
    researcher does become an actual participant in an event or
    gathering, but his participation is determined by his research
    interests rather than by the roles required in the situation he is
    studying. For example, in social gatherings, the researcher
    may try to steer the conversation to topics in which he is
    especially interested.
3. Researcher participates. In this approach, the researcher tem-

porarily abdicates his study role and becomes a "real" participant. After the event, his role reverts back to that of an observer,—and in this case, an analyst of his own actions while being a real participant. [11]

In his study of an Italian community Gans used all the above methods, but because of limited time he found the second to be the most productive. My wife and I also utilized all three, and we too found time a critical factor influencing our approach. At the onset of our stay in the community we were strictly observers rather than participants.

When we joined parish organizations and became involved in various activities our roles shifted: we were now participating as well as observing. But once I began teaching, the shift was more dramatic. I became a real participant, a teacher with duties and responsibilities beyond those of a researcher. And the same was true for my wife; now that I was accepted, she was asked to join various committees and encouraged to be a real participant in parish organizations. Later she was elected president of the choir and took part in planning social functions.

In short, for this study we found the role of "real participant" the most productive. While it was often necessary to analyze our own actions and their effects on situations in which we were involved we did not see that as a problem. Actually, we learned a great deal from how people reacted to what we said and did. But what is important is that regardless of the degree to which we participated, we never stopped being observers.

Although note-taking was out of the question during most of the activities in which we were involved as real participants, we eventually recorded what had happened. Generally speaking, we could recall details of events, since we frequently talked things over before jotting down our notes.

Finally, Gans's point that "even during the most spontaneously real participation [the researcher] can never shed the observer role entirely" is well-taken. [12] For I look back humorously at my attempts to cover shortstop on the men's softball team while trying to scan the bleachers to see which players had brought their families. Unfortunately, my fielding percentage in no way reflects the amount or quality of data I gathered at those games.

ANALYZING THE DATA

By the time I completed collecting data I had accumulated hundreds of typewritten 5 × 8 note cards. I also had extensive files on each of the families interviewed. And included in those were the results of the interviews; notes on what I knew about the family through my involvement in the community; and my observations of the interview itself, including a description of the home and behavior of its residents.

All the data was arranged at first according to the categories on the interview schedule. But it soon became clear that many of those groupings overlapped. Furthermore, somehow a list of traditional sociocultural categories seemed to lack a sense of what was really important in the day-to-day lives of the people. So I went over my notes several times looking for a way to organize them that would best reflect the nature of life in this community. Finally, I decided on a tri-partite division: family, parish, and neighborhood. Perhaps other arrangements would have been as satisfactory but none seemed more real or meaningful at the time.

Once a system for classifying the data gathered had been devised, it was simply a matter of organizing my notes accordingly and writing up the results.

ETHICAL CONSIDERATIONS

During the incipient stages of the research I told many of the people I was studying the history of the parish and neighborhood. I did that because I felt complete candor, that is, my interest in their day-to-day life, would surely have alienated them, making the study impossible. And now at completion I feel that was the correct approach. For in this community, where gossip is pervasive and sometimes vicious, there is a strong sense of privacy and an unwillingness to accept strangers. A researcher who expressed an interest in everyday life here would doubtless be viewed initially with suspicion if not outright hostility. So my plan in the beginning was to talk about a general interest in Polish Americans and a specific concern with the history of the parish and neighborhood.

Once I had become accepted I began to be more open about the study. I told people exactly what I was doing. While I am sure that many are still unclear as to my role in the community, I also know those with whom I was in more frequent contact understand both my purpose and the methods I employed.

For example, during the course of the study I presented a paper on the community at a conference held at Wayne State University.[13] The one member of the parish who was present (I had invited several) agreed publicly with my findings.

Another illustration of how subjects viewed my work was told to me by my wife. She was out one evening with members of a parish women's organization and became involved in a very lively discussion about past and present goings-on in the parish. Since one of the older women seemed to have a wealth of knowledge on that subject my wife suggested that I would be very interested in talking with her in connection with my study. "What would he want with me?" the woman responded anxiously. But before my wife could reply, the woman's daughter, who was also in the group, answered for her:

> Oh, don't you know about him? He's studying us. He just wants to know how we live. You know, how we raise our kids, what we do for fun, what we think about religion, and things like that. He asks a lot of questions, but it's because he wants to know how you think about things.

In general, then, I feel satisfied that some people—not all, of course—knew why I was there and how I was going about my work. That nothwithstanding, I still have guilt feelings when it comes to the whole question of establishing relationships in order to collect data. What makes my approach justifiable, at least in personal terms, is that individuals of the neighborhood were never merely research subjects. They were and continue to be friends whom we would not have met but for this anthropological inquiry.

To protect their privacy I have used pseudonyms for them and for the parish. Thus the people herein are real but, I hope, not recognizable to other members of the community.

On Methods, Motives, and Myths

2

Past Research on Polish Americans

In a recent talk at the Rockefeller Foundation, Robert Coles, the noted child psychiatrist and author, complained about the state of social science research:

> I'm angry that the research that is being done today is so preponderantly survey research, so heavily tied up with questionnaires, and certain types of interviewing, a certain kind of analysis, and also a certain kind of language. What I have against it is not the nature of the research itself, but rather its excessive prominence on the American cultural scene, the seeming monopoly on the word "scientific."[1]

What Coles is getting at is our reluctance to follow the advice of scholars like Robert Redfield, who years ago argued that social science is both art and science:

> It is an art in that the social scientist creates imaginatively out of his own human qualities brought into connection with the facts before him. It is an art in degree much greater than that in which physics and chemistry are arts, for the student of the atom or the elements is not required, when he confronts his subject matter, to become a person among persons, a creature of tradition and attitude in a community that exists in tradition and attitude. With half his being the social scientist approaches his subject matter with a detachment he shares with the physicist. With the other half he approaches it with a human sympathy which he shares with the novelist.[2]

To understand the validity of Coles's criticism we need only consider this: Readers interested in a realistic portrayal of Polish-American community life should ignore the social science litera-

15

ture and turn to such novels as *Pulaski Place* or *The Hero*.[3] Those writings describe American Poles as real people, people who laugh and cry, people who experience joy and sadness. They lay bare a complexity in which those human emotions prevail because the authors delved into the vicissitudes of the human spirit.

On the other hand, researchers appear to have been more interested in the sterile testing of hypotheses and the advancement of social-scientific theory. In fact, Polish Americans have been utilized as convenient subjects for the study of two separate but related problems: social disorganization and the process of assimilation. Thomas and Znaniecki's study is an example of the first approach, and more recent works, like Neil Sandberg's research in the Los Angeles area, is an example of the second.[4] The main consequence of a body of literature based on those concerns, and an absence of the humanistic methodological approach suggested by Redfield, is a lack of knowledge of the true nature of Polish-American communal life.

The present study is an attempt to address that problem. But first it is necessary to look more closely at what others have written about Polish Americans, not to provide an in-depth review of the literature, but rather to illustrate how the methods and motives of social science researchers may lead to an incomplete and sometimes distorted picture of everyday life among Polish Americans.[5] I shall also argue that Polish-American culture—which is something more than a combination of Polish and American cultural elements—has never really been studied. Finally, I intend to demonstrate that what we do and do not know about Polish Americans is in part a consequence of an assimilationist orientation in the social sciences. Mindful of the information contained in the discussion that follows, the reader will be better prepared to critically analyze and evaluate my own findings.

STUDIES ON SOCIAL DISORGANIZATION

The best known and most widely quoted work on Polish Americans is a five-volume study by William I. Thomas and Florian Znaniecki, originally published from 1918 to 1920, entitled *The Polish Peasant in Europe and America*.[6] According to sociologist

Robert Bierstedt that prodigious work "has been called the one sure classic of American sociology."[7] And for Alex Inkeles, it represents "one of the landmarks of sociological research."[8] Thomas and Znaniecki's study is considered important primarily because of its contribution to sociological theory and methodology.[9] Whether *The Polish Peasant* painted a picture accurately representative of Polish-American society and culture at the time of their inquiry is a question that has not as yet received proper attention. Nor has a consideration of that point been germane in shaping the views of most scholars in regard to the overall contribution of Thomas and Znaniecki's effort. The context in which it has heretofore been evaluated clearly emerges in the following comment by Herbert Blumer:

> The purpose of our analysis [an appraisal of *The Polish Peasant*] is not to judge the correctness of the characterization of Polish peasant society given by the authors. Indeed, the materials would not permit the reader to do so.[10]

While Blumer goes on to say that Thomas and Znaniecki "have shown surprising liberality in making generalizations which seem to be very good, but for which there are few if any data in the materials," his critique, and the conference held to discuss it (which included Gordon Allport and George P. Murdock as participants) completely ignores Polish Americans.[11] Thus even though several comments touch on whether the Thomas and Znaniecki work is accurate and representative, they are directed toward the researchers' analysis of Polish rather than Polish-American life.

The decision to evaluate this study without regard to its accuracy in portraying the way of life of Polish peasants—in Europe, in America—is directly related to the authors' motives for choosing to focus on this ethnic group. Thomas and Znaniecki explain how convenience rather than interest guided their choice:

> The present study was not, in fact, undertaken exclusively or even primarily as an expression of interest in the Polish peasant (although our selection of this society was influenced by the question of immigration and by other considerations), but the Polish peasant was selected rather as a convenient object for the exemplification of a standpoint and method outlined in the methodological note forming the first pages of the present volume.[12]

While it is understandable that respected social scientists would evaluate a study in terms of its authors' formally stated objectives, there is no doubt that a disservice was done by not raising questions about the relationship between the researchers' preconceptions and their findings.

For example, Thomas's biases pertaining to Polish Americans are both candid and clear from the comments he made during the discussion that followed Blumer's analysis of his study:

> Another reason for my choice of the Poles was their behavior in America. They were the most incomprehensible and perhaps the most disorganized of all the immigrant groups. This may be illustrated by what the American police call "Polish warfare." A policeman might enter a saloon where there was a noisy crowd of Poles and say, "You men be quiet," and they might subside immediately or one of them might draw a gun and kill him. This was due to the fact that the Pole in America has two attitudes toward authority. One reflects the old peasant subordination to authority. They were called "cattle" by the landlords and submitted like cattle. The other attitude reflects the conception that there are no limits to the boasted American "freedom."[13]

Also, conveniently in behalf of my present contention, Thomas proffers, though inadvertently, insights into Znaniecki's background and occupation that zero in on the latter's regard for the Polish peasants who had immigrated to America:

> He [Znaniecki] was a brilliant young philosopher who represented also the Polish policy of promoting scholarship in the absence of a state and of institutions of learning. Learning and art were patronized extensively by the great estate owners and this was done in part by giving eminent and promising men some civic duties while they pursued their studies. At any rate, Znaniecki was in charge of a Bureau for the protection of Emigrants as to desirable destination and guarding against exploitation, especially in South America. Incidentally, it meant also, as I understood it, keeping the best elements in Poland and facilitating the departure of the remainder.[14]

Let us be clear now on what we know about Thomas and Znaniecki's choice of subject matter and their preconceptions concerning Polish Americans: (1) their decision to study them was incidental if not irrelevant to the methodological and theoretical purposes of *The Polish Peasant*; (2) Thomas was fairly well convinced—and negatively—as to the social and cultural characteristics of American Poles before he even began his study; (3) Znaniecki had at one time been entrusted with insuring that only the "undesirable" elements of Polish society, the very same ones he was about to study, immigrated to America or other places.

Having now reviewed those facts, we can look with more circumspection at Thomas and Znaniecki's findings. Our concern is their picture of the Polish-American community and the degree to which it is representative. We shall also devote some attention to their predictions as to the future of Poles in America, for they are based in part on the theories and methods that made *The Polish Peasant* a major contribution to the social sciences.

The key to those sections that deal with American Poles is based on the concept of social disorganization, "a decrease of the influence of existing social rules of behavior upon individual members of the group."[15] Part three of the study focuses on "Organization and Disorganization in America." It is the disorganization which receives the most attention; chapter titles include: "Break of the Conjugal Relationship, Murder, Vagabondage" and "Sexual Immorality of Girls." The general conclusion of this study is that the Polish-American community is characterized by social unrest, demoralization, and a degeneration of marriage as a social institution. That last finding is perhaps the most significant as far as the authors are concerned, for they see it as a "social danger" leading to demoralization in other areas of life, especially with regard to raising children and maintaining a stable family life. Indeed, they go so far as to suggest that

> However general polygamous arrangements among American Poles may in fact become they must always bear the outward character of clandestine adultery and thus not only be officially marked as signs of general immorality but must actually contribute to general immorality, i.e., to the decadence of individual life organization.[16]

And they conclude by summarizing their position as follows:

> Thus, in general the marriage situation among the American Poles looks quite hopeless when judged by the standards of the permanent and exclusive conjugal bond. Numerous causes contribute to the

progressive dissolution of the monogamous marriage-groups, and there are no important and general reconstructive factors.[17]

But now we have evidence that shakes the very foundations on which Thomas and Znaniecki based their characterization of Polish Americans, shedding light on their inaccuracies as to marriage and family life, as well as the inauspicious future they had predicted for those institutions. Polzin comes to that conclusion after examining the findings of John L. Thomas, Charles O'Reilly and Margaret Pembroke.[18]

Basing his research on a mid-1940s study of marriage conditions in a Great Lakes-area diocese, John L. Thomas had difficulty reconciling Thomas and Znaniecki's prognostication with his own conclusion

> that the conjugal bond is more stable among Polish than among American Catholics of comparable socioeconomic status. . . . Poles had the lowest percentage in which adultery appeared as the main factor in the disruption of the union.[19]

O'Reilly and Pembroke's 1957 study in Chicago supports John L. Thomas's findings. They investigated social disorganization among Polish-American families from primarily peasant backgrounds, most of whom, interestingly enough, were living in Chicago at the time of the Thomas and Znaniecki study. There were no divorces or separations reported among the sixty-eight married Poles included in the sample. Thus, in the following summary O'Reilly and Pembroke agree with John L. Thomas's conclusion that Thomas and Znaniecki were wrong:

> This limited inquiry found that Thomas and Znaniecki's prediction of widespread disorganization was not borne out among one group of Polish immigrants. The group was not characterized by marital instability nor by the loss of family unity. Neither was there any large scale defection from their traditional religion. Although family disorganization undoubtedly affected some Polish immigrants, it obviously did not affect all of them.[20]

If John L. Thomas and O'Reilly and Pembroke are correct, how and why did Thomas and Znaniecki augur a "hopeless situation"? John L. Thomas provides an answer to that question by emphasizing two critical points, as summarized here by Polzin:

First [Thomas and Znaniecki] used the records of the Chicago Legal Aid Society and of the Cook County Court as the basis for their conclusions, without seeking statistical verification of their representativeness, and, secondly, they did not take into account the power of the internalized religious value system sustained by the parish church and the ethnic community.[21]

Based on those findings, it is unlikely, then, that the widespread demoralization and sexual licentiousness presented as typical by Thomas and Znaniecki were at all characteristic of most Polish Americans at the time of their study. While it is true that the external sanctions of the community may have lost some importance, John L. Thomas points out that the internalized sanctions of religion were always cogent.[22]

It is obvious by now that Thomas and Znaniecki's characterization of American Poles was misleading and not representative. Given the authors' lack of interest in Polish Americans as objects of study in their own right, and their negative preconceptions concerning members of this ethnic group, that conclusion should not be surprising.

Next to the Thomas and Znaniecki work, the most widely quoted source on American Poles is a study on Hamtramck by Arthur Evans Wood.[23] Perhaps the best clue to the content of this book is the author's introductory remark that Thomas and Znaniecki's study "makes a peculiarly suitable prelude to subsequent chapters of this volume."[24] And indeed it does, for Wood's chapter titles include "Political Hi-Jinks 1900–1936, "Political Hi-Jinks (continued) 1936–1942," "The Debacle of the School System," and "Outgrowing Delinquency and Crimes." Briefly, the book focuses on selected phases of life in Hamtramck that lend credence to Thomas and Znaniecki's ideas on social disorganization in the Polish-American community, even though Wood would have us believe his study endeavors to "discover the more constructive aspects of community life."[25]

Curiously, then, Wood does the opposite of what he claims are his intentions. He elaborates on the need to look for the positive sides of life and complains that the Detroit newspapers have built a "stereotype of Hamtramck as a city redolent with crime, vice, political corruption."[26] Yet we find that his chapter titles, mentioned above, are based primarily on those very newspaper reports. Later, after many pages of description, Wood goes on to say that what happens in Hamtramck is typical of city government all over America. Here again we see a curious interplay between what the author says and the focus of his study. Wood speaks from both sides of his mouth, as it were.

Wood also suggests that social disorganization in Hamtramck is a result of the cultural heritage of its residents. For example, in discussing a political campaign he tells us that "the following account of some of the incidents will reveal not only what were the issues, but also the political psychology and methods of the Polish people."[27] And in summing up his study he reveals what he considers to be the "cultural heritage" useful in explaining day-to-day life in Hamtramck. His remarks deserve particular attention.

> Other facets of the situation [various aspects of life among Poles in Hamtramck] are revealed by reference to the cultural heritage of Poles, and to certain of their possibly innate qualities as a people. Concerning their heritage we have suggested that the joyous welcome extended to one of their group who returns from a sojourn in a penal institution resembles the attitude in a Polish village toward one who has been imprisoned by the Russians. Also, the phenomenon of coal-stealing, a truly family affair in Hamtramck, recalls the predatory exploits in the manor forests of the Old World. Likewise, the attempt of Polish fathers in Hamtramck to dominate their wives and children in customary ways reflects their patriarchal traditions. The present writer is in possession of a whip taken from a Polish wife-beater by the Domestic Relations Court in Detroit, which had many such trophies, or artifacts, as an anthropologist would call them. Even the political venality of some Hamtramck politicians, though by no means a monopoly of Polish politics, bears out the old Polish saying, "To be a public official means both honor and profit."[28]

Wood further explains what he means by his reference to what is "innately Polish."

> One might interpret their behavior as an innate manifestation of their extreme individualism, their factionalism, their ebullition and love of the grandiose, their savage humor, and their lack of group loyalty, except when pressure is brought upon their group as a whole.[29]

In all, Wood's picture of Hamtramck life is sociologically questionable and incredibly ethnocentric. Yet, as we stressed earlier, next to Thomas and Znaniecki's study it is the most widely quoted source on Polish Americans.

We have paid considerable attention to the works of Thomas and Znaniecki and Wood precisely because their research has been most influential in shaping the views of social scientists as well as the larger society. Indeed, there is a close relationship between how Polish Americans are portrayed in those popular studies and the content of contemporary "Polish jokes."[30]

While inquiries based on an interest in social disorganization have, until now, taken up most of our discussion, it must be noted here that research focusing more specifically on the degree to which Polish Americans are becoming "Americanized" has been far more common.

STUDIES ON ASSIMILATION

In the late 1920s Niles Carpenter and Daniel Katz studied Polish Americans in Buffalo, finding a kind of "cultural dualism"; i.e., while American traditions were being accepted, Polish traditions remained important to the community.[31] Their approach is an illustration of the nature and intent of future studies. Here, the researchers posit the existence of two cultures—one Polish, the other American—and limit their inquiry to an investigation of how Polish Americans shed one culture to adopt the other.

That procedure may also be seen in the work of Peter Ostafin, who compares two Polish communities in Michigan—one rural, one urban—and shows that Polish culture is more likely to survive in a rural area.[32]

Twenty years later Eugene Obidinski measured the acculturation of Polish Americans in Buffalo on several indices, including attitudes toward name-changing and self-identification.[33] He concluded that while the rate of acculturation was uneven, third-generation families were becoming less dominated by the father and therefore more egalitarian. For Obidinski those and other changes meant that Poles were increasingly adopting the American style of life, while traditional values continued to remain important. Thus with a more recent study we see an earlier approach reinforced: one studies American Poles not to focus on their way of life or their world-view, but to determine whether they are becoming American—however that is defined.

Neil Sandberg's research on Polish Americans in the Los Angeles area is in the same tradition.[34] His objective is to answer the following question: "What is the relationship between different generational and social class groups within the Polish community and the salience of ethnicity in each group?"[35] Sandberg's conclusions are (1) while ethnicity seems to be declining over the generations, it is still measurable into the fourth generation; and (2) there is an inverse relationship between social class and ethnicity. Those are interesting findings. Nevertheless, a problem does arise: How is one to measure ethnicity or ethnic identification? Although Sandberg's process includes what he calls cultural, religious, and national ethnicity, it is apparent that his questions are based on a distinction between things Polish and things American.[36] Yet, as we shall discuss later in this chapter, Polish-American culture may be different from both Polish and American culture. In other words, one can be an American Pole with a strong ethnic identity and have little feeling or concern for Poland or things "Polish." Sandberg misses here because he is essentially concerned with measuring the extent to which his subjects are "Polish" or "American."

Stanley Mackun's study is somewhat different in that it attempts to deal with the changing residential patterns of Polish Americans in the greater Detroit area; it is based on the assumption that geographic mobility implies assimilation.[37] His main point is that Poles are becoming Americanized because they are steadily moving from the city of Detroit to the surrounding suburbs. Mackun also feels his conclusion is justified because subjects respond to his question, "Are you a Pole?" by identifying themselves as Americans of Polish descent rather than as "Poles."[38] Yet both notions—geographic or residential mobility and ethnic identification—may have little to do with the sociocultural characteristics of the people involved. For there is no evidence to support the conclusion that living in a suburban area or identifying oneself as a Polish American rather than a Pole is in any way related to whether one is more Polish or more American.

But the crucial issue here is not whether Mackun or other researchers are justified in making generalizations about Polish Americans.[39] Rather it is the context in which their studies were carried out that requires our attention. In other words, what do researchers generalize about? What do they conclude about American Poles?

Generally speaking, researchers studying Americans of Polish descent have been primarily concerned with their absorption into American society and culture. Consequently, the results deal not with the realities of day-to-day life in a Polish community, but with manifestations of Polish or American culture. What that means is that the existence of a Polish-American culture, a way of life distinct from both Polish and American cultures, is a notion that has simply not been considered.

THE STUDY OF ETHNIC GROUPS
IN AMERICAN SOCIETY

A lack of attention to the life-style, patterns of behavior, and values of Poles in America is not something unique in terms of how social scientists have approached the study of ethnic groups in American society. Indeed, as Robert K. Yin has suggested, our neglect of ethnic groups reflects an implicit value orientation in American social science.[40]

That orientation is based on the assumption that ethnic groups in America will ultimately become very similar in terms of their cultural characteristics. To become similar in such a context means adopting an American way of life. And this point of view is symbolized by the notion of a melting pot, as first described by Israel Zangwill in his play of 1908:

> America is God's crucible, the great melting pot where all the races of Europe are melting and reforming! Here you stand, good folk, think I, when I see them at Ellis Island, here you stand in your fifty groups, with your fifty languages and histories, and your fifty blood hatreds and rivalries. But you won't be long like that, brothers, for these are the fires of God. A fig for your feuds and vendettas! Germans and Frenchmen, Irishmen and Englishmen, Jews and Russians—into the crucible with you all! God is making the American.[41]

While Zangwill's God was "Making the American," social scientists were busily studying the process. And that is just another way of saying an assimilationist orientation has characterized American social science.

As Milton M. Gordon correctly indicates, "assimilation is a blanket term which in reality covers a multitude of subprocesses."[42] He goes on to distinguish between two of the most important: "behavioral assimilation" and "structural assimilation."

> The first refers to the absorption of the cultural patterns of the "host" society. (At the same time, there is frequently some modification of the cultural patterns of the immigrant-receiving country, as well). There is a special term for this process of cultural modification or "behavioral assimilation"—namely, "acculturation." "Structural assimilation," on the other hand, refers to the entrance of the immigrants and their descendants into the social cliques, organizations, institutional activities, and general civic life of the receiving society.[43]

And herein above is indeed a crucial distinction. For Gordon himself argues that the existing literature on ethnic groups, including Polish Americans, focuses on their *cultural behavior:* "that is, the question of to what extent the immigrants and their children have taken on the values and behavior patterns of the dominant American culture."[44] Gordon makes the preceding point for a specific reason: to support his thesis that social scientists have neglected the whole process of structural assimilation. That is true, but in stating his case he dismisses a subtle but important issue. The overlooked significance here is not that the literature has focused on cultural behavior, but rather that cultural behavior has been defined in terms of dominant American values and patterns of behavior.

The consequences of such an orientation cannot be overemphasized. For essentially it means that with few exceptions the culture of ethnic groups in America has never been studied. Polish Americans and other white ethnic groups have not been "objects of inquiry in their own right," as Yin points out.[45] Instead, they have been treated as mere repositories of left-over European cultural traits struggling to acquire American culture.

DEFINING AMERICAN CULTURE

But what is American culture? Bennett Berger discusses what he calls "distinctive American types," such as

> Vermont farmers and Boston Brahmins, Southern Bourbons and Tennessee hillbillies, Beatniks and organization men, Plainsvillers, Middletowners, and cosmopolitan intellectuals, to say nothing of teenagers, the jet set, and many, many more, all American, all different, and none probably very eager to be integrated into an idea of "The American" at a level of complexity suitable for a TIME cover story or a patriotic war movie.[46]

Is there, then, a system of values that could be called distinctly or representatively American? Berger doesn't think so, as is clearly indicated by his answer to the important question just posed above.

> The most systematic attempt by a sociologist, that of Robin Williams in his book *American Society*, is foiled by the fact that important groups in American society do not share the 15 or 16 values which he offers as basically American. There is no question that values such as "achievement," "work," "efficiency," "equality," and the rest have played a significant role in creating the quality of American life, but important parts of the lower and working classes (important because of their numbers) do not share them, and important parts of the upper class (important because of their influence) do not share them—although they may affirm them when a journalist is nearby.[47]

If arriving at a description of "American culture" is such an immensely difficult task, as Berger suggests, then how can we argue that ethnic groups in America are becoming culturally similar by adopting an "American way of life"? Logically, we cannot. Yet that is exactly what Gordon is proposing. While rejecting the idea of a "single melting pot," his characterization of American society in the following paragraph bears a striking resemblance to just that notion as far as culture is concerned.

> American society has come to be composed of a number of "pots," or subsocieties, three of which are the religious containers marked Protestant, Catholic, and Jew, which are in the process of melting down the white nationality background communities contained

within them; others are racial groups which are not allowed to melt structurally; and still others are substantial remnants of the nation-ality communities manned by those members who are either of the first generation, or who, while native born, choose to remain within the ethnic enclosure . . . . All these containers as they bubble along in the fires of American life and experience are tend-ing to produce, with somewhat differing speeds, products which are *culturally very similar*, while at the same time they remain structur-ally separate.[48] (My emphasis)

Thus while Gordon does not totally accept the triple melting-pot theory advanced by Ruby J.R. Kennedy and popularized by Will Herberg, he is convinced that the notion of a multiple pot is an accurate characterization of American society.[49] In reality, then, Gordon's approach does not differ significantly from older ideas of the single melting pot. For the salient feature here is the end result, not whether one posits the existence of one or more melting pots. And obviously, Gordon's end result is a culturally homogeneous population, the same product envisioned by those who subscribed to the singe melting-pot idea. So whether one goes along with the single, triple or whatever multiple melting-pot notion is relatively insignificant. What matters, however, is that all those theories re-ject cultural diversity as a relevant factor in American society.

Yet, to re-emphasize an earlier point, the idea of a culturally diverse American society has been rejected without an adequate understanding of our ethnic groups and their way of life. For example, to be concerned with sorting out what is "Polish" and what is "American" about Polish Americans is to neglect the possi-bility that the whole may be greater than the sum of its parts.

That precisely is the point Nathan Glazer and Daniel Patrick Moynihan were trying to make when they argued that

Ethnic groups, then, even after distinctive language, customs, and culture are lost [and here Glazer and Moynihan are referring to patterns of behavior and values from the "old country"], as they largely were in the second generation, and even more fully in the third generation, are continually recreated by new experiences in America.[50]

And that is why Harold J. Abramson concludes that a model of cultural pluralism will provide us with a more realistic picture of

American society.[51] His findings—that American Catholics are a culturally diverse population, and that ethnic differentiation still exists—are powerfully evidential when concerning ourselves with the failure to adequately describe and analyze the realities of day-to-day life among ethnic groups. Certainly they light on the major reason why we lack knowledge on the nature and extent of cultural diversity in our society.

In later chapters I shall be describing the way of life in an urban working-class Polish-American community. My concerns will be with the relationship between a husband and wife and how they raise their children, and the people's attitudes and feelings toward work, religion, their neighborhood, and the outside world. Some of their behavior and values reflect Polish culture; some, the Polish-immigrant experience per se in the United States; and some, that which is common to many Americans from different ethnic groups and all social classes. Yet the total way of life I describe is peculiar to these working-class Polish Americans from this one particular community.

The Setting 3

Detroit is not one of our more attractive cities. An observer has suggested that downtown, boxed in by expressways located beneath surface level, could be compared "to a medieval town surrounded by a moat."[1] But perhaps even more striking is Detroit's naturally flat landscape and an expressway system that snakes through neighborhoods pulling apart communities. If visitors avoid the freeways for the main arteries and drive along Woodward or Grand River Avenues, they are subjected to "a never-ending image of wires, lights, cars, and neon signs merging together into the distance."[2] Thus to encounter what geographer Robert Sinclair calls "the face of Detroit" can be indeed a very stark experience.[3] One is left with the impression that man and nature have conspired to design a city for automobiles, not people.

Detroit's history, growth, and development since the turn of the century have been inextricably tied to the internal combustion engine; residential and spatial patterns have been based on the auto industry's expansion; and everything, from the number of food stamp applicants to the psychological mood of the city, has depended on the number of cars being produced at any given time. For the heart of Detroit has always been the ominous pump of what has evolved today into the "Big Three," its pulse beating at the current rate of production. Which pinpoints why a conspicuous sign overlooking a main expressway, flashing the up-to-the-minute tally of assembled autos, serves as more than just an advertisement of a tire manufacturer; it not only symbolizes but is also a pressure gauge on the very lifeblood of Detroit, if not the country itself.

Yet the city's well-known image—the automobile capital of the

31

world—has obscured the fact that it is one of the most ethnically diverse metropolises in the United States. Immigrants from all over Europe were attracted by a rapidly developing industry requiring both skilled and unskilled laborers. Hoping for a more prosperous way of life, they came. In 1880, as Frank Angelo reports, "the census showed more than 40 nationalities, ranging from 17,292 Germans to a single Greek."[4] And by 1920 nearly 30 percent of all Detroiters were of foreign origin,[5] Poles being the largest group with 20 percent of the total population, followed by Canadians with 19 percent and Germans with 10 percent.[6] Also in that year over half of all laborers and semi-skilled workers employed by the automobile companies were born outside the country.[7] Soon, by 1930, Detroit ranked third behind New York and Chicago in terms of U.S. cities with a high percentage of foreign-born.[8] And although today it still remains ethnically diverse, there are some important changes that have taken place.

Census figures show that between 1960 and 1970 the Black population increased from 22 to 43 percent of the total.[9] But the dramatic change in the proportion of Blacks does not reveal a true picture, for during that same period the total population of the city declined from 1,670,144 to 1,511,482, largely due to a decrease in whites from 1,182,970 in 1960 to 838,877 in 1970, while Blacks went up from 482,223 to 660,428. These, then, are the major demographic changes that have accrued in recent years: (1) a decline in total population; (2) a decline in whites; and (3) an increase in Blacks.[10]

That notwithstanding, 22 percent of Detroit's population in 1970 was of foreign birth or parentage. And, according to census data on foreign stock, the Poles remain the largest white ethnic group with 20 percent of the total, Canadians next with 17 percent and Italians and Germans each following with roughly 9 percent. Yet such percentages provide only a glimpse into ethnic diversity, for data couched in terms of national origin is limited to immigrants and their children; only they are in the category called "Foreign Stock." So third-generation Polish Americans like myself, for example, are not considered members of an ethnic group.

However, now it becomes interesting to examine the 1970 census data pertaining to the mother tongue of Detroit's population.

The Bureau gleaned that information by asking the following question: 'What language other than English was spoken in this person's home when he was a child?"[11] While their query focuses specifically on the past, i.e., when the respondents were children, it is relevant to note that twenty-six languages were listed for third-generation Detroiters, with each of those representing an identifiable ethnic group.

The curious observer would uncover even more by looking elsewhere. At Tiger Stadium, for instance, there is invariably a capacity crowd for the annual Polish-American Night. And the ethnic festivals draw over a million visitors to the riverfront each summer. And even the telephone book discloses a welter of names from around the world, providing evidence that Detroit is very much an ethnic city.

But perhaps the best source of information is published by the Michigan Ethnic Heritage Center in cooperation with other organizations—*Ethni-City: A Guide to Ethnic Detroit.*[12] It deals with unusual facts not to be found in official reports of the Census Bureau, nor in many sociological studies, such as listings for ethnic churches, organizations, agencies, restaurants, markets, bakeries, and so on. A few of the many nationalities included are Albanians, Chaldeans, Croatians, Estonians, and San Marinese. In all, there are over sixty ethnic groups. Having completed a brief overview of ethnicity in Detroit, we shall turn to the purpose of this study, to examine one of those groups—the Polish Americans.

POLISH AMERICANS IN DETROIT

In 1870 a delegation of Polish immigrants came to Casper Borgess, the German-born Bishop of Detroit, seeking permission to organize the city's first Polish parish.[13] Until then, Poles in Detroit had been attending mass at two German-Catholic churches, St. Mary's on the corner of Antoine and Monroe, and St. Joseph's on Gratiot between Riopelle and Orleans. But the steadily growing Polish population was no longer satisfied with that arrangement. They wanted a parish of their own: a church where they could worship within the framework of their cultural heritage, and a school where they could educate their children and maintain that heritage.[14] They desired a pastor of their own, a Polish priest who would not only provide spiritual guidance but who would be especially equipped to give practical advice for dealing with the problems of adjusting to a new way of life.

Bishop Borgess listened intently to the Polish immigrants, though with cautious interest. His main concern, according to the official history of St. Albertus, was the financial burden of constructing and maintaining a church.[15] But the delegation was insistent, and some time later the bishop reluctantly agreed to their request.

The first few years of the parish were marked with financial difficulties, but the determination of the parishioners prevailed; St. Albertus church, Detroit's first Polish parish, was officially dedicated on July 14, 1872.

But there was more to St. Albertus than just a parish. It was a community that included most, if not all, of the Polish immigrants in the city. As Thomas and Znaniecki have said,

> the Polish parish is much more than a religious association for common worship under the leadership of a priest. The unique power of the parish in Polish-American life, much greater than even the most conservative peasant communities in Poland, cannot be explained by the predominance of religious interests . . . the parish is, indeed, simply the old primary community, reorganized and concentrated. In its concrete totality it is a substitute for both the narrower but more coherent village-group and the wider but more diffuse and vaguely outlined "Okolica." In its institutional organization it performs the functions which in Poland are performed by both the parish and the commune.[16]

Thus it is not surprising that the territorial concentration of Polish immigrants began in an area immediately adjacent to St. Albertus church. The influence of the parish becomes all the more important when we consider that the church was located on the northeastern edge of the original Polish settlement, on the corner of St. Aubin and East Canfield.

As Mackun has shown, the new parish soon became the center of an expanding Polish-American settlement:

> The Polish church exerted a centripetal force on the growth of the settlement. Shortly after St. Albertus Church had been built, the

Poles began to buy property close to the church and expanded the settlement.[17]

As the expansion continued between two main thoroughfares (to the west Woodward Avenue, to the east Gratiot Avenue), influencing the residential patterns of Polish Americans, it had a definite effect on the spatial distribution of many other ethnic groups in the city. St. Albertus parish was the core settlement of Polish immigrants on the east side of Detroit; St. Casimer parish attracted Poles on the west side. Our concern here is with Polish Americans on the east side of the city.

They are no longer clustered around St. Albertus parish, which is now a predominantly Black area. Having moved, they expanded their settlement to where their center of population is closer to the northern suburb of Warren than to downtown Detroit. Still, Polish parishes continue to serve clearly identifiable ethnic neighborhoods. And St. Thaddeus, the focus of this study, is a prime example.

ST. THADDEUS PARISH

St. Thaddeus was formed in 1925 by a group of Polish immigrants who lived in a section of the city whose parish was not Polish. It did not cater to the needs of American Poles: sermons were in English, and confessions couldn't be heard in Polish. Nor was there a parish school that could educate their children while maintaining their cultural heritage and traditions. As we have shown with the early settlers who organized St. Albertus, there was a great desire among these people for their own parish and school. So they too petitioned the bishop and were granted permission to establish what is known as a national parish, one that serves a specific ethnic group rather than a territorial area.[18]

A Roman Catholic parish, strictly speaking, is a formally organized structure with a recognized leader whose authority is clearly defined within a system of norms and values based on ecclesiastical regulations. According to canon law the purpose of a parish is "the cure of souls."[19] Therefore, its official function is to fulfill the religious needs of parishioners. Yet parishes also perform important social functions and develop an informal structure above and beyond canonical requirements.

The aforesaid is the key to understanding St. Thaddeus. For it is a Polish parish, and as we have learned earlier from Thomas and Znaniecki, a Polish parish in America is "simply the old primary community, reorganized and concentrated."[20] That Thomas and Znaniecki were referring to Polish parishes of the early 1900s hardly alters the significance of their statement, as we shall soon see.

St. Thaddeus parish buildings include a church, school, rectory, and convent. There is also an activities building that houses a gymnasium and a cafeteria, and is used as a meeting place for parish organizations. Between the school and the convent is a small grotto highlighted by a statue of Our Lady of Częstochowa, the patroness of Poland, along with two rows of votive lights and a set of kneelers for visitors. Those structures plus the parish parking lot take up two city blocks.

To determine the exact size of Catholic parishes in the United States usually presents a problem, and St. Thaddeus is no exception. So while it is impossible to precisely number the membership, among whom are both adults and children, we do know that St. Thaddeus has twelve hundred individuals who regularly contribute to the financial support of the parish.[21] Since most of them are heads of families, total parish membership is probably more than three thousand.

Like all other Roman Catholic parishes, St. Thaddeus has a formal structure or plan of organization. And that structure as Donovan describes it, is essentially "a system of positions occupied by persons with the lines of authority and communication drawn between them."[22] The pastor, a second-generation Polish American in his early fifties, is the official head. He is responsible for how the parish functions, both spiritually and administratively.

The two curates (priests who assist the pastor) at St. Thaddeus are subordinate to the pastor in administrative power, status, and prestige. In terms of formal structure the nuns who teach in the parish school rank between the curates and laity. They are directly responsible to the pastor, though held in lesser rank than clergy in the eyes of the Catholic church. At the same time, "the formal

expectation of their personal sanctity and the fundamental importance of their teaching or other roles to the parish and the church
reward them with a prestige rank superior to that of the laity."[23]
In the organizational structure of St. Thaddeus, parishioners
represent the lowest strata:

> They are expected to acknowledge the religious authority of their
> pastor and priests in matters of religion specifically, to follow their
> spiritual leadership, and to live in conformity with the dictates of
> God and His church.[24]

Parishioners do have their role on the administrative side of parish
life through the parish council, a body consisting of lay persons
elected by their peers. Although the pastor heads the council, he
looks to it for advice and guidance in his ministration. He makes
the final decisions on matters of importance to the parish, for he
alone is responsible to the bishop for its condition, both spiritually
and administratively.

In addition, the parish also has other units that may be properly
considered substructures within the larger system. The first is the
parish grade school, a social system in its own right. Its principal,
a nun, is directly responsible to the pastor.

The second is what may be referred to as the "associational
structure," which includes all parish societies and organizations,
such as the Holy Name Society and the Altar Society. In total,
there are fifteen, each with specific goals and elected leaders. But
those who belong are parishioners first and society members second. Their leaders are responsible to the pastor, so parish organizations are considered a part of the formal structure.

Now we can plainly see that the formal structure of the parish is
a highly organized network of interacting units with a specific
purpose and a clearly defined authority structure. In short, the
parish is a social system whose formal structure is designed primarily to fulfill the religious needs of parishioners. However, in the
course of performing tasks associated with goal-oriented activities
an informal structure emerges based on spontaneous sentiments or
feelings.

One aspect of that is the real rather than the ideal relationships
among the levels or strata in the parish. In other words, while the

pastor is the official head according to the formal organization, a young assistant could have more authority or status because he is well-liked and a strong personality. But this is not the case at St. Thaddeus; it is only an illustration of how the realities of parish life are not always reflected in its formal structure.

But relationships along the lines of stratification in the parish, ideal or real, are not my main concern here. Actually, I am primarily interested in the nature or form of the informal structure that exists among parishioners.

That structure is a network of nuclear families.[25] Some are in direct contact while others are not. So this is not a situation where "everybody knows everybody else," but rather where "everybody knows somebody who knows somebody else." These nuclear families are linked together directly, or indirectly through participation in the formal structure of the parish.

THE NEIGHBORHOOD

The network of nuclear families just described has significance above and beyond its relationship to the formal structure of the parish, for most of the families who belong to St. Thaddeus live in the same residential area, an area surrounding the parish.

I arrived at my conclusion from an analysis of parish records and the R. L. Polk City Directory for Detroit.[26] A record of registered parishioners was checked against a listing of residents in the area, according to the Polk directory. The results show that over 70 percent of all households within a specific locality have individuals who are members of St. Thaddeus parish.

Pursuing the matter further, I plotted the spatial distribution of parishioners on a large map of the general area surrounding the parish.[27] I found that 71 percent live within the same specific locality. While a small cluster of parishioners reside just outside that area, the remainder are distributed among other sections of the city and suburbs.

The locality under discussion is the census tract in which the parish is located; a majority of parishioners reside within the boundaries of that tract. But what really needs to be emphasized now is that my finding is related to the above discussion of the parish as a network of nuclear families. It is now possible to identify a section of the city that becomes more than just a series of residential streets with rows of houses; a large segment of the network of nuclear families is localized in a defined geographic area.

That area is what I shall call a *neighborhood*, a locality with "physical boundaries, social networks, concentrated use of area facilities, and special emotional and symbolic connotations for its inhabitants."[28] Its limits are based on the spatial distribution of parishioners; and its network of nuclear families represents the informal structure of the parish. In fact, all member families are a part of the network regardless of where they live. But our concern here narrows to that segment which is localized in the area referred to as a neighborhood.

Residents there are emotionally attached to it and the parish. They feel at home because they know one another, and because the total environment fulfills both their religious and social needs. Such an ambiance symbolizes what it means to be an urban working-class Polish American: an individual whose life revolves around the family, the parish, and the neighborhood.

Interestingly enough, the parish and neighborhood are closely identified as a unit both by its members and outsiders. "I live *in* St. Thaddeus," a parishioner and neighborhood resident would likely say to those from other sections of the city. And in turn he would likely be understood in Detroit, for St. Thaddeus is indeed an identifiable social and geographical unit.

The growth and development of the parish is synonymous with that of the neighborhood. Even though it is difficult to show that the formation of the parish was directly responsible for the growth of population in the subject neighborhood, it is significant that those who settled there in the 1920s were Polish Americans. From interviews with some of them I learned that the presence of a Polish parish in the area, including a school, was a crucial factor in their decision to move here. So St. Thaddeus acted as a magnet, drawing Polish Americans.

We have defined the area as a neighborhood, a locality and a social fact. It is St. Thaddeus parish, I have suggested, that is a source of social organization for the neighborhood. So here we have two separate yet related social units. And while it is possible

to analyze the parish and neighborhood separately, in reality they
function together to form a community.

THE COMMUNITY

The term community is admittedly a conceptually ambiguous
one, but at present there is no better word to describe adequately
the social phenomenon that is the parish and neighborhood.[29] For
here is clearly a situation where the whole (what I have called the
community) is greater than the sum of its parts (the parish and
neighborhood).

Roland Warren has identified five major functions of any community: (1) production, consumption, and distribution; (2) socialization; (3) social control; (4) social participation; and (5) mutual
support.[30] And now, perhaps the best way to illustrate my point
that the parish and neighborhood form a community is to examine
the extent to which they perform those functions.

In regard to the first function—production, consumption, and
distribution—it is obvious that individuals must leave the neighborhood in order to earn a living. Moreover, much of the money
earned is spent on goods and services that have little to do with the
parish and neighborhood as a social unit. That is true even though
people contribute to the parish, pay their children's tuition in the
parish school, and do some of their shopping at local commercial
establishments. However, since individuals are dependent on the
city for their economic survival, the parish and neighborhood do
not constitute an autonomous economic unit.

But the parish and neighborhood are very important in terms of
socialization, the second major function. Warren defines socialization as

> The learning process through which individuals, through learning,
> acquire the knowledge, values, and behavior patterns of their soci-
> ety and learn behavior appropriate to the various social roles which
> their society provides for.[31]

He also emphasizes:

> It is on the local level that individuals encounter the culture and
> social systems of the larger society and are inducted into these sys-
> tems and acquire the appropriate attitudes and behavior patterns.[32]

In the situation I describe, the "local level" is the parish and neighborhood, a setting which provides children with their first opportunity to encounter a world larger than their own family. It is within that setting that they acquire the knowledge and skills necessary to function in society. But perhaps more important is that a child's personality is shaped in this milieu as he internalizes the values, attitudes, and beliefs of others into his conception of self. And the formation and development of individual personalities is an important dimension of the socialization process.

That is significant, for many social scientists have pointed out the close relationship between personality and culture. And I have suggested that the way of life in the subject parish and neighborhood represents a distinct set of cultural patterns. The network of social relationships supported by the parish, including its church, school, and organizations encompasses a significant part of a young child's world. His life and the lives of most adults revolve around the family, the parish, and the neighborhood—and in that order. Thus a youngster is not merely learning about society as an abstract construct. He is learning how society is viewed by the members of his family and others who participate in the world of the neighborhood and parish. How he views that society, and how his own personality is shaped by the way of life in the community, is not our concern in this chapter. Rather, what I have tried to demonstrate is that the parish and neighborhood are a powerful and significant force in socializing children.

The same is true with regard to social control, Warren's third major function. Social control may be defined as "the process through which a group influences the behavior of its members through conformity with its norms."[33] An important part of that process is the period of socialization: i.e., when individuals acquire feelings about what is right and what is wrong. Their feelings—"I ought to do this" or "I ought not to do that"—express internalized norms, and norms are what Judith Blake and Kingsley Davis have called "the cutting edge of social control."[34] As S.F. Nadel suggests, when norms are internalized there is very little need for organized social sanctions on the part of a group or community.[35] So in such a situation social sanctions are usually diffuse, in the form of gossip or ridicule, praise and blame and ostracism.

Those describe social control in the neighborhood with which we are concerned. Later, I will describe how even the physical appearance of the neighborhood reflects an internalized norm regarding cleanliness. The fact that people who fail to conform to that norm are the subjects of gossip and ridicule rather than organized social sanctions is evidence of the degree to which social control is dependent on internalized restraints.

The attitude toward cleanliness is part of a Polish American's social heritage. But many other attitudes and beliefs are more directly related to the role of the Catholic church in the socialization process. So far I've been emphasizing the parish in terms of its social functions. However, as John Thomas has argued, Polish immigrants and their descendants have internalized the sanctions of the Catholic religion to such a degree that their attitudes and values are closely related to what the church teaches.[36] So the church is still a powerful influence in the lives of Polish Americans through the development of internal sanctions that affect their attitudes, beliefs, values, and patterns of behavior in the areas ranging from sex to politics. And in addition to those the social life of the parish and neighborhood has its own sanctions on various aspects of behavior. In summary, then, the parish performs both social and religious functions that serve as a strong source of social control in the subject neighborhood.

Warren's fourth major function is social participation, the opportunity to interact with others in different ways.[37] With fifteen organizations, ranging from a senior citizen's club to a cub scout pack, the parish certainly provides that opportunity for all age groups. Indeed, it is the center of social life for those who live in the neighborhood. Socializing among neighbors and friends takes place primarily at parish social events and activities, not in the home. So, it is participation in the parish that establishes and maintains the network of nuclear families who reside in the neighborhood.

Mutual support is the fifth and last function of any community according to Warren. He defines mutual support as

the type of help which is proferred in those instances where individual and family crises present needs which are not otherwise satisfied in the usual pattern of organized social behavior. Examples are

illness, economic need, and problems of family functioning. . . .
Mutual support may be roughly characterized as "providing help in
time of trouble."[38]

There are several reasons why the parish plays an important role in
performing the functions of mutual support as Warren has defined
it.

First, there is the traditional role of the pastor in both Europe
and America. Generally speaking, he is a person who is looked to
for more than spiritual leadership. In Poland the pastor was often
the only educated person in the community, and people looked
up to him as a leader in both religious and practical affairs. To
an extent that tradition has prevailed in Polish-American communities. For example, when a crime is committed the victim
will call the police and then, the pastor. So he, as we see, is
expected to help in times of trouble. He is viewed as the leader
of the community.

Another reason the parish is important in terms of the fifth
function is related to the cultural attitude toward assistance from
social service agencies. To apply for food stamps or Aid to Dependent Children is considered shameful by many residents. It implies
that an individual cannot handle his own problems, that he has
been defeated. That point of view is based on the belief that
problems are the result of personal failings, like not working hard
enough, rather than societal forces. Moreover, social assistance is
viewed as "getting something for nothing," an attitude that dis-
courages the needy from seeking help because it would be denying
a more basic need: self-respect based on tangible accomplish-
ments. In other words, there is a basic value conflict here between
the prevailing point of view that "nobody owes me anything" and
social assistance as "getting something for nothing."

Thus mutual support or help in time of crisis must be skillfully
offered lest it be declined or lead to a loss of friendship between
donor and recipient. The pastor and his curates are skilled in that
manner, and somehow practical assistance from spiritual leaders is
interpreted differently from that offered by social service agencies.
The church should care for its members, and the pastor should be
concerned about his parishioners. So here again we see how the
role of the parish is important in the lives of the people.

The third reason the parish is important in performing the function of mutual support is related to its role in establishing and maintaining a network of social relationships in the neighborhood. Notwithstanding the cultural attitudes and values mentioned above, there are times when people need and request help from others. Relatives are usually asked first, and then the pastor and his assistants. But often one need not request assistance; it is offered by fellow members of the social network, which represents the parish and neighborhood.

Let us now sum up our findings on the functions performed by the parish and neighborhood. We have found that together they perform four different functions: socialization; social control; social participation; and mutual support. Only the economic function— production, consumption, and distribution—has little relevance as far as the parish and neighborhood are concerned.

Raymond Breton has suggested that ethnic communities (and here he is speaking of a network of individuals and groups, not necessarily a locality group) often try to provide for all the requirements of their members.[39] That means in addition to a network of social relationships ethnic communities have developed an institutional framework that supports the community in order to fulfill its needs, religious, social, and educational. Together, St. Thaddeus parish and the surrounding neighborhood form such a community.

Now obviously here we do not have a community in the strictest sense of the word, for it is not autonomous. People must leave it in order to earn a living, see their physician, and carry out numerous other tasks. But it fulfills so many other needs of its members that it is perhaps best viewed as a community. That approach emphasizes the degree to which the parish and neighborhood form a social and geographical unit culturally distinct, a world of its own where people spend a great deal of their time.

This, then, is a contemporary urban Polish-American community. It is a social reality, a social form with which we are relatively unfamiliar. Thomas and Znaniecki brought it to our attention more than fifty years ago, but we failed to recognize it then, and we have failed to trace its persistence up to the present day. That such a community still exists is in itself strong evidence of cultural diversity in American society, for as Conrad Arensberg and Solon Kimball point out,

> There will be an American community . . . for every American culture. Indeed, conversely, for as many types of communities as we can distinguish from the record there will be so many cultures upon the American scene.[40]

What I am suggesting here is that the particular form of community just identified is representative of working-class Polish-American culture in Detroit. Future studies can demonstrate the extent to which those findings apply to Polish-American culture in other urban settings. Here we can only make a beginning, an attempt to describe and analyze one particular community.

The members of the community in question belong to three separate but related social units, the family, the parish and the neighborhood. I have described how the relationship among those units represents the structure of the community under scrutiny. But before examining the realities of day-to-day life within each unit it is necessary to describe the physical and demographic characteristics of the community. The unit of analysis here is the census tract— what I have referred to as the neighborhood—which includes both St. Thaddeus parish and the majority of its parishioners.

AN OVERVIEW OF THE COMMUNITY

St. Thaddeus parish is a Polish-American neighborhood in the northeast section of Detroit fifteen minutes from downtown, via expressways, and ten minutes from the suburb of Warren, via surface roads. So the neighborhood is located almost midway between the suburbs of Detroit to the north, and the city of Hamtramck to the south. The western fringe of the Italian section is located directly east, while the west is an area populated by Polish-Americans and Blacks, primarily the latter.

To mention the word city in the present decade is to conjure up images of urban slums, run-down tenement districts waiting for the bulldozer, and an inhospitable environment becoming increasingly unfit for human beings. But those are not the characteristics that describe this neighborhood. In short, it is a very pleasant place to live, a section of the city that has managed to maintain some of the more positive elements of life in an urban setting. Its narrow tree-lined streets are lined with rows of one-story wood-frame houses that seem more attractive now than they were more than forty years ago, when most of them were built. They have been improved, not just maintained. In addition to frequent coats of white paint many owners have added aluminum storm windows and cement porches with wrought-iron railings. Others have enclosed their porches or constructed a spare room on the rear of the house. Some sections of the neighborhood contain brick homes, and they too are tidy and attractive. But besides the excellent condition of the homes, the appearance of the neighborhood is enhanced by carefully manicured lawns and tiny backyards with statues of the Blessed Virgin amidst colorful flowers and intricately arranged vegetable gardens. The same care that is lavished on the home is extended to the lawn and backyard.

Even the streets are clean. Homeowners feel responsible for the portion of the street in front of their property. Hence it is not unusual to see a housewife sprinkle the pavement with her garden hose and then sweep it clean with a strong broom.

The physical characteristics of the neighborhood are related to the cultural attitudes and value of its residents, especially their need for order and cleanliness. While the neighborhood takes no action on a formal level, people who fail to keep their houses and property in excellent condition soon become the target of gossip and ridicule. But such cases are rare, for the majority willingly conform to the unwritten rules. Indeed, they feel uncomfortable when "things aren't as they should be," i.e. neat, clean, and in perfect order.

For example, one woman told me that her neighbor's garbage was continually in a state of disarray, and "the alley looked like hell." So she proceeded to clean up her neighbor's mess and continues on a regular basis "so the alley will look nice and neat." Now in such a situation gossip and ridicule obviously had no effect on the neighbor who neglected the physical appearance of her alley. However, her neighbor was so uncomfortable with the situation that she felt compelled to take action herself. Yet the two women had never discussed the issue. Here is an example of how norms for order and cleanliness have been internalized to such a degree that they become psychological needs.

The general attitude I describe applies to the inside of the home as well, perhaps even to a greater extent. For the home is considered sacred, almost like a shrine, and cleanliness is a sign of respect. Mothers and daughters are thus faced with a never-ending task: to keep the inside of the home spotless and in perfect order. The floors are not merely wiped with a sponge mop, they are scrubbed on hands and knees with a tough bristled brush. The dishes are not only dried, but polished until they shine. Spring cleaning is not an annual event; it is an activity that goes on from day to day, all year round.

Years ago many of the people who lived in the neighborhood spent a great deal of time in their basements. That way it was easier to keep the rest of the home in order and reserve a place for entertaining friends and relatives. While that is no longer true, some of the homes still have basements that reflect the old pattern. Prospective buyers are astonished when they descend the stairs to the basement and encounter wood floors, plastered walls, and full kitchens. But they would not be quite as surprised if they understood that living in the basement reflected a concern with cleanliness, an attitude of pride and respect toward the home, and a feeling that all available space should be fully utilized. In one way or another all those attitudes and feelings are reflected in the lives of people who reside in the neighborhood at the present time. Later in the study we will explore just how that is so. But now let us return to describing the neighborhood in terms of a place to live.

In addition to the residential streets there are thoroughfares that serve as its northern, southern, and eastern boundaries. The commercial establishments, which cater to the needs of its residents, are located mainly along the northern thoroughfare, which is a four-lane city street with one additional lane on each side for parking. Traffic is heavy most of the day, and many trucks use the street as an access route to the nearby expressway.

It is important to emphasize here that although this thoroughfare is part of the neighborhood, in a sense it is more a part of the city. For once you leave the residential streets of the neighborhood you enter a world where the faces and and cars you see are no longer familiar. In the neighborhood itself you know people, the cars they drive, and you know where they are going at various times of the day. But the city street is filled with strangers who view the neighborhood merely as a section of the city one passes through on the way to or from someplace else. So in a psychological sense the city street represents a departure from the familiar world of the neighborhood and an encounter with the strange and unfamiliar world of the city. It is in this way that the city street is a part of Detroit rather than the subject neighborhood.

Yet the commercial establishments serve both the residents of the city and the neighborhood, though most seem to cater to one or the other.

A small diner, formerly a drive-in, is a meeting place for delivery men, telephone and gas company employees on repair runs, and police officers from the nearby precinct. Truck drivers also stop because of the convenient parking area. The short-order cook and two waitresses all speak Polish to one another but English to their customers. The food is good and inexpensive, and includes daily specials like kielbasa, pierogi, and gołąbki. Seemingly, very few of the customers live in the neighborhood, with the exception of teenagers who stop for cokes and hamburgers.

Another restaurant stands two doors from the diner, and it caters to a different clientele. Larger, it seats around seventy people. And residents of the neighborhood eat there occasionally with their families. Still, most of the customers are businessmen passing through, or office workers from nearby tool and die shops. The prices are higher and the menu is more varied, including pizza and barbecued spareribs. Some Polish food is served, but not on a regular basis. And only one of the five waitresses is a Pole. So in contrast to the small diner one hears very little of the language spoken.

In addition to the two restaurants there are numerous other commercial establishments that cater to residents of the city rather than the neighborhood, including a gas station, a radio and electronic supply company, and three corner bars. A large greenhouse and flower shop is also located on the thoroughfare and it too draws customers from all over Detroit, though local residents purchase flowers there when the need arises.

Then, there are four establishments that derive almost all their profits from the neighborhood. Probably the most important is Johnny's Market, a relatively small, family-owned supermarket known for its fine meats, availablity of credit, and friendly manager who knows more about community gossip than most of its residents.

Johnny knows every customer by name. He encourages you to tell him about yourself and your family, and goes about it in a friendly and sincere way, appearing to be genuinely concerned about your welfare as an individual not a customer. And as a result of his approach, he is a storehouse of information, and his market has become an institution in the neighborhood. Even though prices there are higher than in the large supermarkets, many people use his facility for all their shopping. For each visit to his store provides an opportunity to learn of various things, such as how Mrs. Jaworski recovered from her operation, or whether the police caught the thieves who took Mr. Karaszewski's color TV set.

People also shop at Johnny's because they know that if they are out of a job or laid off he will give them credit, no questions asked. In short, his market, as an institution, seems almost ancillary to the parish.

The two bakeries, which sell fresh dark bread and various Polish pastries, are also important, but mainly because of their products, not as centers of neighborhood life. Still, the availability of those items lends character to the neighborhood and provides evidence of its continuing viability as a settlement of Polish Americans.

No place ethnically imbued would be complete without a funeral parlor: this is the fourth establishment that deals primarily with neighborhood residents. Like the supermarket, it too is family-owned, and while the original owner is no longer alive, the business is carried on by his son. The relationship between the funeral parlor and the neighborhood has always been close. The director is a Polish American and he understands the customs and needs of the people. In a sense the funeral parlor is an extension of the parish, primarily because death to Polish Americans is a time when the role of the church is of utmost significance. For in addition to the last rites and the funeral mass itself, there are also rosaries said for the deceased at the funeral parlor and a service at the cemetery. Thus people in a given area and parish tend to identify with a specific burial establishment much as they do with a specific church. The significance of such an attachment becomes evident when many people, having left the area, still express their desire to be buried from their former parish and neighborhood funeral parlor.

So far I have been describing the commercial establishments lining the city street that serves as the neighborhood's northern boundary. None of the other boundaries is as important in terms of establishments that meet the needs of local residents. The eastern boundary, for example, is also a four-lane city thoroughfare, but much busier than the one we have just detailed. The firms located there are all of an industrial nature: small tool and die shops; a factory that manufactures steel beams and wire fences; a warehouse for an aluminum siding and awning concern; and numerous other enterprises that can be classified as small industries. Few if any of the local residents are employed there, nor do they perceive those firms as part of the neighborhood. In a sense that ends as one approaches the eastern boundary. For in addition to industrial firms located on the thoroughfare, there are railroad yards beyond, so the area is not a residential district, but more like an industrial park.

The southern boundary, again a thoroughfare, though not as large as the other two, has only one establishment, a small corner grocery store. It caters mainly to the residents who live in the predominantly Black public housing project located across the street.

There is very little contact between residents of the neighborhood and those of the housing project, making the city street both a physical and social boundary. Local residents view the project with fear and resentment: they say it is a place to avoid out of concern for your physical safety, a place where people without jobs survive through welfare and the social service system, which operates by taxing those who work to support those who don't. Such attitudes and feelings on the part of neighborhood residents are quite enough to preclude any interaction with the people who live in the project. But also important are the views of the Blacks; they see the neighborhood as a bastion of white racism, a place that is predominantly white because of a concerted effort to keep them out. Later, we shall learn how the attitudes and perceptions of both groups fail to reflect the realities of a much more complex situation. But for now it suffices for us to know that the eastern boundary is effective in a geographic as well as a social sense, and that is unimportant as far as commercial establishments are concerned.

The last point is also true for the western boundary, a residential street that does not appear to have any significance as a dividing line that helps to mark off the neighborhood. But in reality quite the opposite is true, for all the boundaries are based both on census tract divisions and the spatial distribution of parishioners. So the residents to the west of this avenue belong to another census tract and a different parish. They are not members of the St. Thaddeus community.

Since our focus for the remainder of the study is on the way of life in the subject community, it will be helpful here to review some of its demographic characteristics.[41] U.S. Census figures show that the total population of the tract in question is 3,474; 1.6 percent of whom are Black. Residents who fall into the category called "foreign stock" constitute 56 percent of the total population. Of those who are considered "foreign stock," 37 percent are foreign-born while the remainder are second generation. And over 75 percent of all individuals in the category are of Polish ancestry.

With regard to age, 30 percent of the total population are 55 years and older, and 25 percent are under 15. Of those 25 years and older 32 percent have completed high school; the median number of school years completed is 10.1.

Of all employed males, 75 percent are blue-collar workers, most of whom labor in Detroit's automobile factories. Nearly half of all of them are craftsmen, foremen, and kindred workers. The median family income from wages and salaries is $11,381.

The majority of homes in the neighborhood—60 percent—were built before 1939, and 50 percent of all residents in 1970 had lived there more than twenty years. And the median value of all homes is $13,400.

The Family 4

This chapter explores family life in the context of the immediate social environment. It begins with a description of how husbands and wives relate to their friends, neighbors, and relatives, followed by a consideration of married adults as partners and as parents. My approach is based on the advice of Elizabeth Bott, who suggests that our understanding of a family's internal structure will be enhanced through learning about its social environment.[1]

WOMEN AND FRIENDS

Friendship among women in the subject community is characterized by a desire for intimacy on the one hand, and fear of self-disclosure on the other. Twenty married women were asked to describe the qualities they looked for in a good friend. Their responses were strikingly similar, as illustrated below:

> To me a friend is someone who will listen to what I have to say and keep her mouth shut. Many of the women around here betray your confidence by telling all your secrets. I don't need that kind of friend.

> I like people who don't "knife you in the back." But most of the women in this parish seem to enjoy doing just that.

> The most important thing about a good friend is that she must be honest and not talk behind my back.

> A good friend is someone who is my friend to my face as well as behind my back. I know, because I've been burned many times. People just seem to live to talk about me. I wouldn't mind it so much if they just had the courage to say what they had to say to my face.

53

So now we can see how women of the neighborhood want close friends with whom they can share "secrets," but are wary of establishing such intimate relationships, and for a very good reason: there are few secrets in this community. People gossip to the point of viciousness, at social gatherings in the parish activities building, on the church steps after Sunday mass, in front of the meat counter at Johnny's Market, from nearby porches as the morning mail is collected, and over the back fence while the day's wash is being hung to dry.

Nothing is sacred as far as the contents of those conversations are concerned. If a couple is having marital problems people will talk, like when I overheard several women at a parish dance.

"Did you know that she refuses to sleep with him?" the first began.

"That's been going on for months," said the other woman.

"Well, they've been married for twenty years and haven't spoken to one another in the last two, so what can you expect?" the third chimed in.

Yet the gossip is not always so intimate. Indeed, more common are judgements about a woman's abilities as a housewife and mother. To illustrate, the following are comments directed at two different individuals.

I dropped by last week at two in the afternoon and would you believe that she was still in her bathrobe. No kidding! And the house?—why, it was a mess. Beer cans on the floor, ashtrays all filled with cigarette butts. Yet there she was having a cup of coffee and reading the paper in the middle of that mess.

She's not strict enough with the kids. I guess she and her old man just don't give a damn. The little one sasses her and the teenager gets the car all the time and stays out as late as he wants. It's no wonder the kids don't do well in school. What would you expect, coming from a family like that?

The fact that women gossip tells us a great deal about day-to-day life in this community. But we must take care in explaining why it is common and what purpose it serves. Too often it is viewed just negatively, as "small talk," or what's worse, "idle chatter." Clearly, it is much more than that.

The term "gossip" was originally a positive one, applied to close friends or relatives, people with whom you were especially intimate. As Alexander Rysman reminds us, the word

> developed out of the Old English as a contraction of the phrase "God sib" and referred to the relation a family would have with someone they felt close enough to to make into a god-parent for one of their children. Just as the "d" in "God's spell" dropped to form the word "gospel," so "God sib" became "gossip."[2]

While the meaning of the term has changed through the years, even today people must know each other quite well in order to engage in gossip.

Indeed, a folklorist who studied an upper middle-class community has called gossiping "a form of sociable interaction," and suggested that "the content of the talk is not as important as the interaction which the talking supports."[3] Polish-American women who meet, however briefly, to exchange information about members of the community under discussion are in fact socializing.

They are also articulating standards of proper behavior for wives and mothers, husbands and fathers, and children and relatives. Those standards reflect shared values and beliefs and provide people with direction and guidance in their everyday lives. Through gossip, then, norms are stated, values are reaffirmed, and conformity is maintained.[4]

But there is a price, and women are most often asked to pay it. They must guard against being accused of spreading rumors and gossip, as well as protect themselves and their families from becoming targets of tittle-tattlers and thus the "talk of the town." So we see now that women in this community have a somewhat difficult lot. They are curious about the private lives of others, desirous of close friends with whom to share their "secrets," and, at the same time, must be fully aware of what can happen if they are too curious or too friendly. Moreover, on a personal level, they seem to enjoy the gossiping while concurrently feeling guilty about it. One woman very candidly described those feelings:

> I know I gossip too much, and I know it's wrong. But you know something funny? When I gossip about so and so for not being a good housekeeper I realize that I'm better than she is. And I feel

pretty good about that. Of course I feel guilty about gossiping so much. After all, it is a sin. But nobody praises me for what I do, so maybe this is one of the ways I get my kicks.

Until now we have been discussing some of the factors that influence patterns of friendship among women. Here we turn to a consideration of how attitudes and feelings toward friendship, and norms and values governing the role of housewife, may affect patterns of socializing. Again, my information is drawn from responses to a question regarding the characteristics of a good friend. Women told me what they looked for in such a person, but they also revealed something about themselves and their daily lives:

> Well, I like people who don't complain. But what really bugs me is when they want to come over to the house. I don't like people who bother you—who feel they have to see me often or talk on the phone. You don't need that much contact with people. They interrupt your housework and make you feel like you're wasting time.

> Friends shouldn't make pests of themselves by dropping in all the time, especially when I'm cleaning the house.

> I don't like folks who have to see you real often. They disrupt my housework. And that disrupts my whole life. I just don't feel right if the house isn't spotless and the dinner isn't ready. When I want to see a good friend or talk with her I'll let her know it. When I need her help I'll ask for it.

Socializing during the day is therefore seen as bothersome and disruptive, primarily because of cultural rules in regard to how women should spend their time. To defy those norms is to invite criticism for wasting that time, for not being a good housewife, for not having the home in perfect order.

While all homes are spotlessly clean, and dinner is always on time, maintaining such standards is not something women consciously discuss among themselves. In fact, when I commented to several housewives about the importance of cleanliness and order they were quite surprised at my observation. "Yeah, I guess it's important," one of them said, "but I never realized it until now." Another agreed, and then added:

> I'm miserable if someone drops in and my house isn't spotless. I feel I'll be the laughing stock of the neighborhood. But it's not just

that I worry what the neighbors will say: it just makes me uncomfortable when the house isn't as it should be. I guess I kinda feel out of sorts if there is work to be done.

Given the value placed on orderliness, in terms of the home's physical appearance and running the household, there is always work to be done. Thus women of the community are busy, very busy; visiting during the day is out of the question.

But despite those constraints, and the fear as well as the ambivalence surrounding gossip, women do have close friends with whom they share innermost thoughts and feelings.[5] However, friends who are considered "close" one month may not be speaking to each other the next. So alliances are constantly shifting, broken by betrayed confidences, established with renewed hope, and always entered into with caution.

Participation in parish events, activities, and organizations provides the opportunity to form friendships. Women are more involved in the parish than the men. Their organizations outnumber those for adult males, have a larger membership, and are more socially active.

For example, if a woman is a member of the Madonna Guild or the Altar Society she may attend a "Ladies' Night Out." Those are group trips to a nightclub, theater, or dinner and the movies, with the association picking up part of the expense. There are also card parties and special luncheons specifically for women. Weekly bingo games are popular too, and each Thursday evening nearly three hundred ladies are in attendance. The men's organizations sponsor a few social events for their members, but they are not as frequent nor as well-attended.

Women who belong to the parish organizations are more likely to choose their close friends from within the community. And while socializing in the home is a fairly rare occurrence, daily chats on the phone—often lasting a half hour or more—are very common. So the proverbial grapevine in the subject community is a network of women who belong to parish organizations. Gossip travels, first, through those groups—via monthly meetings, social events, and the telephone—then radiates throughout the larger community. Thus ladies who are active members constitute the core or nexus or the overall network that links all the families in the parish.

There are some who refuse to join, fully aware of the function organizations in the parish perform. "Not me, I wouldn't sign up," said one forty-year-old mother of two. "Why, those nitpicking women get together just so they can gossip. And if you miss a meeting you known darn well who they will be talking about. I tried it once. Now I just want some peace and quiet." While those who feel that way tend to choose their friends from women who are not members of organizations, they are still linked, albeit indirectly, to the network we have described.

In addition to leading a more active social life than males, women play a larger role in parish affairs. They are the key organizers, the individuals responsible for insuring that parishioners work together on various activities, like raising money for the school or other worthwhile causes. Although sometimes they work behind the scenes, women constitute the majority on the school board and parish council. And when they speak, the men—including the pastor—listen.

Women command respect because they are seemingly more articulate than the men. While the latter tend to be reticent in group situations, the former are outspoken and far from timid. And in public wives appear to have better social skills than their husbands.

In the light of those considerations and the foregoing discussion, it should be clear why women are responsible for establishing and maintaining the network of nuclear families in this community. Their role, however, will become even more evident as we begin to examine friendship patterns among men.

MEN AND FRIENDS

Women refer to their close friends as "girlfriends," "ladyfriends," or "pals." But the men have no comparable terms to describe those with whom they are very familiar. There are "buddies," "guys," and "boys," but they refer to companions, not intimate friends. A man goes to a baseball game with his buddies, bowls with the guys, and stops for a beer with the boys. He does not share his inner thoughts and feelings—his private life, that is—with the fellows. The above notwithstanding, do men have close friends? I asked, and the following are two quite typical answers:

> Well, that's a pretty tough question. Because you see, I'm really involved with my family and job. I guess I don't have much time for friends. And now that you ask that question I guess I'd have to say that I don't really have any close friends. Oh, I like the guys at work all right, but they don't come over to the house or anything like that. I don't see them outside the shop.

> I don't have any close friends, to be perfectly honest with you. I know a lot of guys from the parish and the shop. And they're nice guys, don't get me wrong. But we're not all that close. Hell, when that whistle blows I want to get home as fast as I can.

Some replied differently, and even named one or two individuals. But they rarely saw or socialized with them, most of whom were "fellows from high school" or "guys I grew up with." One forty-nine-year-old screw machine operator put it this way:

> Well, I used to be pretty close with Steve and Al. But that was before I got married. We went to high school together and had a lot of fun playing ball and chasing girls. But I don't know, once we got married we went our separate ways. I wonder whatever happened to those guys? One of these days I'm gonna give them a call so we can all go out for a beer and talk about old times.

Before marriage, so it seems, men do have friends they consider close. With a wife and family, however, things are not the same. There is a job, a house payment to meet, food to buy, and children to raise. And leisure time is spent at home with the family: watching television; playing with the kids; or putting a fresh coat of paint on the house.

Out of twenty men interviewed, only three spend "an evening out with the boys" once every two months. Two go deer hunting once a year with the guys from the shop and two others bowl weekly in an organized league. Thus most evenings are quiet ones at home.

But when men do get together their conversations are markedly different from those of a woman and her friends: there is baseball rather than recipes on the agenda, and new Buicks instead of new wallpaper. Those are obvious contrasts. However, more subtle, yet of greater importance, men talk less about themselves. After a few beers, one might say, "Christ, it's been a bad week what with the old lady getting sick and my boss giving me hell," but then the conversation shifts to another level, and everyone seems relieved. For complaining about problems, especially those that affect one personally, is viewed as a weakness. It is wives who *talk* about problems, the men say, and the husbands who *solve* them.

Yet it would be misleading to say men never discuss their feelings. They do. But not with other men, which is characteristic of many adult males in American society. As Lillian Breslow Rubin has correctly pointed out, "to the degree that the American culture approves male expression of closeness or intimacy, it is between a man and a woman, not between two men."[6]

Perhaps that explains the striking differences between husbands and wives in terms of what they consider important in choosing a close friend. You will remember from our earlier discussion that women stress such characteristics as the need to "keep secrets." Men, on the other hand, emphasize shared interests and similar attitudes. Here three individuals speak for themselves:

A good friend is a guy who thinks like me. You know, he likes what I like and and he hates what I hate. You gotta be able to talk about sports, politics, things like that. If you always disagree then you ain't friends.

I don't like guys who are always ready to argue about everything under the sun. A close friend is a fellow you agree with, someone you can talk to.

Close friends are hard to find. You don't feel comfortable with just everybody. There has to be something there. And I don't know what it is. Maybe it's people like you, people who think the same about most things.

So we see here that men define friendship differently than women. The need for psychological intimacy is not mentioned, although agreeing, feeling comfortable, and being able to talk, are. Is it possible, then, that intimacy is viewed dissimilarly by males and females? Perhaps Rubin, a female sociologist, considered that question when one of her male colleagues insisted she was wrong about the lack of intimacy among working-class men. She quotes their conversation:

"I've heard any number of guys confiding their problems to a workmate," he argued.

"What kinds of problems," I asked.

"For example, they'll talk about the fact that their car is a lemon," he answered.

"You call that intimate talk?" I asked.

"Sure," he answered, "in the sense that the guy reveals something about himself and his lack of judgement in getting stuck like that. It threatens his manly image, the pose that he can always take care of himself, that nobody can get the best of him."

"Granted," I replied, "but does he tell his workmate that he's worried about his sexual performance; that he has nightmares that his wife might leave him; that he's just found out she's having a love affair with another man? That's the kind of sharing I'm talking about. It's of a different order than the things you call intimate."

"Okay, I get your point," he answered. "We *are* talking about different things when we use the word 'intimacy.' Of course, the guys I'm talking about don't talk about those very personal things to each other."[7]

But despite the dissimilar views of men and women on that issue, as in the foregoing dialogue, the fact remains that in the particular community under discussion adult males *say* they have no close friends. Furthermore, my observations support the generalization that they do not share personal feeling with one another. We may conclude, then, that however friendship and intimacy or closeness are defined, women have confidants, while men do not.

Yet there is male camaraderie: at a poker game after the Dad's Club meeting; during a softball game; or at a golf outing. But a man's job and family responsibilities are taken seriously, and leisure time outside the home is a luxury that most cannot afford, financially or in terms of time. Finally, and perhaps most importantly, men do socialize. But they prefer to do so in the company of their wives, at parish social events, or holiday gatherings with relatives, and not exclusively with other men.

NEIGHBORS

Immediate neighbors play a relatively insignificant role in the day-to-day lives of husbands and wives in this community. For despite residential propinquity, social homogeneity, and mutual participation in the parish, relationships among neighbors are characterized by an absence of visiting in the home, minimal socializing out-of-doors, and respect for one another's privacy. A "good neighbor" is one who keeps to himself except when needed by others.

While women interact more than men, there are no coffee klatches. One longtime resident tells why:

> No, housewives around here rarely drop in on each other for a cup of coffee and a chat. When that starts women get in each other's hair by gossiping about whose house is in better order, who is still in her bathrobe at nine in the morning, and so on. Besides, we're too busy to waste time on useless chitchat when we have our dishes to wash, floors to wax, and meals to prepare.

So rather than socialize in the home, women converse while watering the lawn, hanging clothes to dry, getting the mail, shopping in local establishments, and walking to and from morning mass. Those encounters are brief and unplanned. And that's the way it should be; women say, "It's the family that counts." The following is how the home and family-centered theme is expressed by a woman describing her immediate neighbors:

> They're nice people—they keep to themselves and don't bother us. This is the way it should be, because we all have families, and taking care of them is a twenty-four-hour job. Oh, I like the people around here pretty much but we kinda have an unwritten agreement. They keep outta my hair and I keep out of theirs. We talk when we meet each other but we're careful not to interrupt one another's housework or be bothersome in any way. That's how we all manage to get along so well. We know each other. And we all know how we feel about our homes and families.

Husbands spend most of their day away from home and therefore have fewer opportunities for contacts with neighbors. Still, patterns of interaction are somewhat similar. Men nod and greet each other while watering the lawn or working on the car, but lengthy conversations are rare. Occasionally, a person will help his neighbor repair a car, lay sod, or move a heavy piece of furniture. But that is an exception to the rule.

To the casual observer, then, it appears that neighbors hardly know each other. Yet nothing could be further from the truth.

The houses in the subject neighborhood are very close together, so close that by standing on your porch and reaching out you can almost touch your next-door neighbor's. So when the weather is warm, and windows are open, conversations can be heard and arguments cannot be ignored. Furthermore, one family knows the other's schedule or daily pattern of activities, and the slightest deviation will become a topic of conversation. "Something is going on at the Jakubowski's," one woman will say to her neighbor as they wait for the morning mail. "The old man was two hours late from work last night, and little Julia didn't show up for school this morning. I'll bet George is hitting the bottle again," she will conclude from her observations.

Neighbors also know who visits whom. "The Skorupski's have company," children will shout to their parents when they see a familiar car pull up in front of a neighbor's home. "Ma, I think it's their grampa," one of the kids will say. "Isn't he the one who drives that 1973 blue Chevy with the dent on the left side?"

But observation is only one of the ways residents learn about one another. Participation in parish organizations also provides the opportunity to gather information, as already mentioned. Another source is through children who attend the parish school.

For boys and girls tell their parents about goings on in the classroom and the principal's office. If Mary comes to school sloppily dressed, is sent home for misbehavior, or is failing English, her classmate Johnny will tell his parents. And because Mary lives across the street from Johnny, his mother and father become aware of their neighbor's "problem." On the other hand, if Johnny is a model student his neighbors will be sure to know. Indeed, Johnny's parents may acquire social status in the community, based, of course, on what children have told their parents.

It is important, however, to consider more than what people know about one another in order to understand day-to-day life in this neighborhood. Of utmost significance is the fact that there is a social bond among neighbors. For example, if someone's house is burglarized his neighbors will come over not only to console but to help repair broken windows and damaged doors. And older people need not worry about mowing their lawn or shoveling snow. A younger neighbor will do it without being asked, and expect nothing in return.

Thus relationships among neighbors here are characterized by what a sociologist has called "latent neighborliness."[8] People are friends without being friendly, and except when others need help, "they keep themselves to themselves."[9] Those patterns of behavior serve to emphasize the importance of the nuclear family through minimizing outside social contacts.

RELATIVES

Studies concerned with the way of life among the urban working-class emphasize the importance of extended kinship ties as a source of close interpersonal relationships and as an influence on behavior.[10] And blue-collar neighborhoods are often viewed as social units based on "relatively extensive kinship networks reflecting traditional kinship lines."[11] Yet in this community families differ considerably with regard to the nature and extent of their contact with relatives. And while some families have relatives who belong to the parish and live in the neighborhood, the overwhelming majority do not. Clearly, now, we see that this community is not a localized kin network.

Although it is generally true that some families see their relatives primarily on special occasions, others interact frequently and intensively. It is possible to explain the varying degrees of social distance between families and their relatives by considering the following factors: a family's stage of development, the physical accessibility of kin, and immigrant generation.

Usually, young husbands and wives who have children of preschool age tend to maintain an intimate relationship with their parents. When a family is at that stage of development a husband and wife are dependent on their parents for babysitting, advice on child-rearing, and, more often than not, financial assistance. Moreover, the relationship between young children and their grandparents is at a peak then. The latter are curious about the growth and development of their new grandchildren and excited about being called "Gramma" or "Grampa." The warm feelings that develop between young children and their grandparents serve to insure that young marrieds will spend more time with their own parents.

But things begin to change once the children enter school. Now, babysitters are drawn from the pool of teenagers in the neighborhood and the young wife is confident in her ability to be a good mother. The need for financial help is also less important, for the young husband has had time to establish himself in a job and save a little money. By the time all the children are in school the husband and wife tend to see their parents less often, and the focus shifts from extended family relationships to an emphasis on the nuclear family. Of course if there are marital or job problems young couples will remain dependent on their parents.

As the children continue on through school they see their grandparents and uncles and aunts on special occasions like First Holy Communion, birthdays, graduations, and during the Christmas and Easter holidays. Occasionally, a husband and wife will visit their parents on a Sunday afternoon when the weather is warm and the family feels like going for a ride. And there are always phone conversations. But at that point of development socializing with relatives is often viewed as a duty and obligation rather than a form of mutual enjoyment and pleasure.

It is interesting to note that spending time with relatives is considered bothersome by many families at this stage because it tends to de-emphasize the nuclear family. One father in his early forties expressed his feelings on the matter:

Holidays can be a real bother. We have to see her parents, my parents, and all our brothers and sisters. So we end up spending half the day in the car, traveling from one place to the next. It's nice to see the relatives, but I have my own family now and it would be nice to stay at home and celebrate the holidays in a quiet way. But what happens around here is this: we don't see members of our family that often during the year, then when holidays come we try to pack in all the socializing in one or two days. For me it's become a real hassle. But I don't think it will change.

Another problem for many people is the dilemma of choosing between the wife's or husband's relatives. "We spent last Christmas at your mother's," a husband will say to his wife, "and Christmas Eve at mine. So this year we had better reverse things, or I'm going to raise hell." There is no hard and fast rule governing which side of the family you see when, or perhaps more importantly, most often. Consequently, debates on that issue are frequent and heated, and the final decision is often unsatisfactory to all parties concerned.

We can generalize, however, about patterns of interaction between families and relatives. Because most adults in this community have children of school age or beyond, frequent contact with parents and siblings is not customary. But there are two important exceptions.

The first involves families with relatives in the immediate neighborhood.[12] Husbands and wives in that category stay in constant touch with their relatives through all the stages we described earlier. They see each other more than once a week, have daily phone conversations, and, generally, are friends as well as relatives.

Families who emigrated from Poland after World War II also differ from the majority. Here again, regardless of the stage of development or physical proximity, husbands and wives remain on intimate terms with their relatives. For the 20 percent of the people in this community who are recent immigrants, then, extended kin ties are significant. Indeed, to that segment of the community relatives are their only friends. While most of the first-generation Polish immigrants have parents who still reside in Poland, their siblings and cousins live throughout the Detroit metropolitan area. Visiting with those relatives, both formally and informally, makes up their social life.

We should also mention here that the recent immigrants are not really a part of the subject community in a social sense. They attend mass and send their children to the parish school, but rarely attend parish events and functions. And to my knowledge, a post–World War II immigrant has never joined a parish organization. Finally, for various reasons, interaction between recent immigrants and other members of the community is practically non-existent.[13]

To sum up this section, we have learned that the majority of families are oriented toward the nuclear family. Their relationship with relatives is intimate while the children are of pre-school age, and sometimes beyond, but soon after the independence of the nuclear family is stressed. Families with relatives in the community and recent immigrants are the exceptions to those generalizations.

How important, then, are friends, neighbors, and relatives to most of the members of this community? A second-generation father explains as follows:

> We live in a world of our own and like it. Sure we attend social gatherings at the parish and we never miss an athletic event when one of our kids is involved. And we see relatives on birthdays, graduations, and holidays. But we rarely get together with our friends and neighbors. We keep to ourselves, I guess you could say. This is the way we like it. After all, just how important are other people? It's the family that counts, and when you have a close family you don't feel the need to be with other people.

HUSBANDS AND WIVES

One way of gaining insights into the husband-wife relationship in any culture or community is to probe into how married partners characterize the ideal spouse. With that in mind, I asked husbands and wives the following question:

> Suppose for a minute that a nephew/niece of yours came to you for advice in choosing a wife/husband. What advice would you give in terms of the kind of person he or she should look for?

Without exception, men stressed the importance of choosing a woman who was interested in family life and capable of being a good mother. Below are the words of three respondents:

> Well, the main thing I would tell my nephew is to look for a girl who likes her family. And there are ways you can find out, like asking her what she thinks of her mother and father and watching how she treats her brothers and sisters.

> You gotta like the girl, of course, but it's easy to be fooled by her looks or what she's like on a date. The real question is: What's she like at home? Because a young man must never forget that this woman he is dating is going to be a mother for his kids.

If you had asked me that question when I was twenty I would have said that it's important to choose a woman whose measurements are 38-24-36. But now I know better. What you've got to look for is a woman who knows how to handle children. And that takes a woman who grew up with a mother who knew how to handle her. Hell, I know now that beauty and brains aren't all that important. What matters when you're together for a long time is the kind of family you have. That's what I'd tell my nephew, but he probably wouldn't listen anyhow.

He should make sure the girl comes from a decent family where everybody respected everybody else. Because once you get married the girl will behave the same way she behaved in her home. If her mother was a complainer, she'll be a complainer. If her mother mistreated the kids, she'll mistreat the kids. So you gotta find out how she behaves around her own family. That's the most important thing.

While it is noteworthy that men describe the model spouse primarily as a mother, it would be misleading to conclude husbands view their wives solely in the context of that role. Rather, their responses reflect a concern with the difficulties of raising a family, the hopes and dreams they have for the children, and the knowledge that it is the wife who assumes major responsibility for managing the household. In short, men are not de-emphasizing the wife as a partner, as some middle-class observers might presume. They are articulating a family-centered point of view.

Women express a similar attitude when portraying the ideal husband, by stressing the significance of work. "There are a lot of things I could say," remarked a thirty-seven-year-old mother of four, "but the most important thing is that a young man must love to work." Other wives agreed:

You know, it's tough to give advice to young people these days because they think they have all the answers. But if my niece actually did ask me for help I'd tell her to find a hard-working man who wasn't afraid of work. He ought to be willing to work overtime, too, because that's what really helps the family.

I'd tell my niece to look for a guy who's got a job that can support the family. And he better be the kind of a guy who can keep the job. Forget those guys who go from one job to another because they hit the bottle or because they're just plain lazy. Give me a guy who loves to work and everything else will take care of itself.

Why do women feel that way? Simply because they have lived through years of financial insecurity and constant struggles to make ends meet. Sometimes fearful, usually uncertain, but always skillful, women have managed. Barely. And that is the emotional climate of working-class families in our society, a kind of "economic trauma," if you will.[14] A factory worker's salary is not meager, but it is never enough to preclude the anxiety that comes with contemplating the present and the future. And often, families come to depend on overtime pay just to make it through the month. So the lack of that as well as the possibility of "getting laid off" are constant fears. And the men combat those trepidations the only way they know how: by working hard at their jobs, accepting overtime when it is available—and through it all they refrain from complaining.

Women know, then, that their family's very survival depends on a husband who "is not afraid of hard work." And thus, when describing the characteristics of an ideal spouse, wives are in fact reaffirming the value of the family as a social unit. They are also telling us how difficult it is to subsist economically.

Middle-class wives respond differently when asked "what they value in their husbands," according to Lillian Rubin, who conducted a comparative study:

> They tended to focus on such issues as intimacy, sharing, and communication and, while expressed in subtle ways, on the comforts, status, and prestige that their husbands' occupation affords. Janet Harris, writing about middle-class women at forty, also comments that she never heard a woman list her husband's ability to provide or the fact that he is "good to the children" as valued primary traits. "The security and financial support that a husband provides are taken for granted," she argues; "it is the emotional sustainment which is the barometer of a marriage."[15]

But, as Rubin correctly argues, among working-class families "the material aspects of life are problematic, and . . . *never* 'taken for granted.' "[16] Mindful of that, we cannot assume that the women in the subject community are disinterested in their husbands as lovers or confidants. Nor should we suppose that a man is

expected to play a minor role as a parent. But more on those topics
in a moment. At this point I'd like to include additional material
on the ideal spouse.

We focus again on what husbands consider desirable in a model
wife:

> You gotta remember that a woman has to be willing to sacrifice.
> You get married to set up a home and that's a lotta hard work.
> Sure, you and your wife can go out to the movies when you first get
> married, but once them kids come along she has to be willing to
> stay at home. The good times are over.

Indeed they are, as two more husbands assured me:

> She's gotta be neat, both in the way she dresses and in the way she
> keeps the home. If she's neat and tidy she'll set a good example for
> the kids. And you know what keeping a neat home means? I'll tell
> you. It means sacrificing. Because she's not going to be able to
> spend time gossiping with the women or going out to those demon-
> stration parties. She should stay at home.

> Raising a family is an expensive proposition. It means that a
> woman has to sacrifice. She can't have new clothes as often as she
> likes, and she can't go out as often as she likes. That doesn't bother
> me as much, because I don't need that much in the line of clothes,
> and I'm content to stay at home and watch TV. But a woman, hey,
> she had better be ready to sacrifice.

So, both husbands and wives view marriage and raising a family
as being hard work. While the men are more explicit on that
point, the theme of "sacrifice" permeates through how each sees
the other's role. For the man "who loves to work," and who is
willing to spend countless hours of overtime at the plant, the
sacrificing seems just as much to him as to the woman who is
forced to spend evenings at home or do without a new outfit.

But more pertinent to our discussion of husbands and wives is
how that motif—the need to sacrifice—influences their relationship. For example, when marital problems arise the general attitude
is that it is best to "suffer" than seek professional help. And, here, I
am not suggesting that serious marriage difficulties represent a pattern in the community. I am merely saying that when they do exist,
efforts to solve the problem through outside assistance are rare.

There is, of course, an aversion to psychological counseling in general, but that is not an important point at the moment. Rather, I am concerned with the attitude that marital problems are "a cross to be borne," and something one should expect:

> When I got married I thought I had a deep love for my husband. Now I know differently. Getting along with him on a day-to-day level is one helluva trial. But I make it. By God I make it. I go to church. I pray. I go to communion regularly. And it all helps, I guess. After all, we are in this for life.

> You know, I answered your question about choosing a husband and I meant what I said. But let me tell you something. Really, you don't have to know that much about a man, just make up your mind that you can live with anything. Most of us women didn't really know our husbands before we married them anyhow. So what a woman needs to do is be ready for anything. That's what makes for a successful marriage.

Women are not alone in the posture just described. For men with domineering wives who criticize their every word and movement also believe that an unpleasant marriage must be endured. "Come hell or high water," said one man, "it's forever. So you live with your mistake, and there's nobody that's gonna make things different. Besides, marriage is a private thing between you, your wife—and the Almighty. And that's the way it is."

Divorce is out of the question, even though few people agree with official church policy on the matter.[17] A mother of three teenage youngsters explained her position, with which most others agreed:

> If two people can't get along they should be allowed to get a divorce and not be penalized by the church. But personally I'd never even consider it, no matter how bad things got. I could never live with myself. And then I'd feel guilty about the kids. But if someone else wants to do it a priest shouldn't get in their way.

But what about most marriages, where problems are not serious and man and wife get along fairly well? To help fill in our picture of this community, let us first look at the relationship between husbands and wives in working-class Italian-American families, as described by Herbert Gans, a sociologist:

The marital relationship is qualitatively different from that of the
middle class. Not only is there less communication and conversation between husband and wife, but there is also much less gratification of the needs of one spouse by the other. Husbands and wives
come together for procreation and sexual gratification, but less so
for the mutual satisfaction of emotional needs or problem solving.[18]

None of the above is true for Polish-American couples. Husbands and wives talk a great deal, usually after the children are in
bed. They discuss finances, plan for the future and remember the
past. And they talk about themselves, too. A wife is intimately
acquainted with her husband's work situation, and often proffers
advice on how to deal with a difficult boss or a workmate who is
not carrying his load. And in turn a woman does not worry alone.
She tells her husband about problems with the children, and he
listens. Then jointly they decide on a plan of action, a way of
dealing with the situation. While it is the wife who is primarily
responsible for raising the youngsters and managing the household, her husband is expected to demonstrate concern with those
matters.

Casual observers sometimes make presumptuous judgments
when it comes to the emotional aspects of married life, especially
if they are of a different social class from those whom they are
studying. But the relationship between a husband and wife is a
private one, whether they live in a rural African village, an urban
community, or a bedroom suburb. So we must take care when
characterizing a marriage, among Italian or Polish Americans
alike.

And, of that I am certain: My wife and I came to be friends of a
number of couples during our three-year residency in the subject
community, and we fail to see significant differences between the
emotional side of their marriages and those of our middle-class
acquaintances. Gans suggests an absence of marital closeness
among the Italians he studied.[19] And others tend to accept that
characteristic as a pattern of all working-class marriages.[20] But, on
the basis of my experience, I would argue that marital closeness is
culturally defined. And so is love, to an extent. What matters is
that partners agree on the rules of the game, so to speak, even if
those rules remain unstated, unarticulated.

Now let us consider the flexible division of labor between husband and wife. I have mentioned several times that women assume major responsibility for running the household and caring for the children, yet that is not a rigid arrangement. When a wife has a job, her husband shares those tasks.[21] For instance, if a woman is employed in a factory and works the day shift, who prepares the breakfast, gets the kids off to school and makes the lunch and dinner? The husband, of course, who also straightens up the house before working the afternoon shift.

Men are also good cooks, and take pride in preparing special dishes. But they don't talk about it. Nor do they discuss how often they do the food shopping, or look for sales and coupons in the daily papers. Our distorted image of the Polish-American blue-collar worker doesn't prepare us for the various roles he is willing to take. Therefore, as objective observers, we must learn to distinguish myth from reality. And that only comes from experience, from getting to know people. Like the left fielder on our softball team who would phone to tell me of our next game, and then ask, for example, if I'd seen page 34 of *The Detroit News*, where A&P was advertising chuck roast for only 69 cents a pound! At first I was surprised, but later I learned to take notes when he called, soon running off to the supermarket, checkbook in hand, a bargain my goal.

All in all, then, marriage is a partnership. While it may differ in some respects from that of middle-class couples, one would be presumptuous to say it varies greatly with regard to how people feel about one another, or to make judgements about the degree of closeness.

There are misconceptions about another aspect of the husband-wife relationship in working-class marriages. For the literature leads one to believe that it is the husband who makes all the important decisions, who has the "veto power," and it is the wife who is left to say "He won't let me."[22] But in the Polish-American families I came to know the realities of day-to-day interaction between husband and wife are much more complex.

First, contrary to public opinion, Polish-American women are not Edith Bunkers who bring their Archie his beer and slippers while waiting timidly to be told what to do next. Instead, they have a great deal of authority. And, as wives and mothers, they are a source of strength and wisdom to other family members, including their spouses.

The wife is also her family's business agent and representative to the outside world. She pays the bills, manages the budget, makes appointments with doctors and dentists, and lodges complaints with department stores or supermarkets for faulty products or poor service. Highly competent, always efficient, and never submissive, a Polish wife is an excellent family manager. And at times, she does not hesitate to tell her husband what to do. For example, one woman admitted to me that her husband was reluctant to be interviewed for this study, but dismissed his concern with the following remark: "You come at 7:00 P.M. on Monday night and he'll be here, whether he likes it or not. And don't you worry. I'll take care of everything, and it will be okay. Or he'll answer to me."

A seventh-grade student of mine in the parish school also provided some clues about the marital relationship when he explained his mother's role:

> Ma helps us out. She explains things to Dad. You know, she makes it sound better than it is, like sometimes she doesn't tell Dad the whole story when we do something wrong. This is great for us, because sometimes Dad won't listen to us. But he listens to Ma, or else he'll be the one who's in trouble.

I asked couples about the decision-making process, and both husbands and wives agreed "it is a fifty-fifty proposition, with the man having the edge." Yet through observation one learns that interviews can be misleading, that there is a difference between what people *say* and what they *do*. For often it is the wife who suggests it's time to look for a new house, that a new color TV is too much of a luxury, that her husband needs a new suit. And while those matters are jointly discussed, it would be wrong to assume that the wife plays a submissive role. In fact, she gets her way often enough that we may forever lay to rest the myth of the second-generation Polish-American husband as an authoritarian figure who maintains absolute power over his wife. Nor should we believe that Polish-American women are timid, inarticulate, and afraid of their husbands. They are not, and their husbands know it.

But women are reluctant to admit they have attained a position of power within the family. They would prefer to say, as I suggested earlier, that "men have the edge." And understandably so, for to do otherwise would cause serious marital conflict over the traditional male role as head of the family, and disrupt the emotional climate of family life. In a very real sense, then, the power of women rests on their maintaining that image.

We must recognize that the marital relationship described above represents a dramatic shift from the patriarchal authority system which characterized family life among Polish immigrants in America in the early 1900s. It is also important to keep in mind that, so far, our discussion has focused on couples who are second-generation Poles. But, as we mentioned earlier, 20 percent of the total population in the community presently under scrutiny came to the United States after World War II. Those recent immigrants are first-generation, and it would be instructive to examine their marital relationships to illustrate generational change and difference in life-style between two groups in the same community.

In first-generation immigrant families there is a very strict division of labor. The husband does not assist his wife with domestic tasks such as washing the dishes or doing the shopping, and he refuses her offers to help with the painting or repair work around the home. While leisure time is spent together, it is primarily because most socializing is done in the home with relatives. As was pointed out, both husbands and wives in first-generation families have few friends outside of relatives.

But what is perhaps more conspicuous is that the father, here, dominates his wife and children and makes all the important decisions. He views his wife as the mother of his children, a person who takes care of the meals and laundry for the family's benefit. And when husbands and wives have problems, they tend to discuss them with relatives rather than with each other.

Still, there is a large measure of agreement on the norms of immigrant family life. Husbands and wives are in accord with their respective roles, except for one major point. While the women are willing to take jobs to help support the family, their husbands are adamant about their remaining in the home "where they belong." And although several women do have jobs cleaning offices or washing dishes, their husbands are very dissatisfied with this arrangement. For those men feel others will say they are unable to support their families, a crushing blow to the recent immigrant.

We have already described how the division of labor is more flexible in second-generation families. But men of the first-generation who observe women from those families painting the front porch and exterior trim are horrified. "That's women's work?" they say. Watching a man changing a diaper or giving the kids a bath would also evoke such a response. Yet that is not to say that all second-generation men regularly become involved in those tasks, but their wives do request that help, and those who acquiesce are viewed as good fathers.

Among recent immigrants a wife will not ask for assistance in domestic matters. It would be tantamount to admitting she couldn't handle the responsibilities of motherhood, and that is something she would never do.

Let's return for a moment to the question of women working outside the home. Quite frankly, all men in this community would prefer that their wives not work. Second-generation husbands, however, are more flexible, especially because they realize that when a wife works the family benefits by affording things otherwise unobtainable. One man, a father of four, put it in the following manner:

> Hell no, I'm not happy about my wife working, especially in a factory. I'd like to be able to support the family on my paycheck. Oh, I suppose we would make it on what I earn. But just barely. Now that the wife is working we bought a color TV and we're going to get a new car. And we don't have to worry so much about putting the kids through school and buying them clothes. I'm not happy about it, but it's a helluva lot easier this way.

Now there are families in which the wife is employed in an office or a factory and still assumes major responsibility for domestic tasks. But she expects her husband to help out and criticizes him when he doesn't comply. That is not as common in a family of recent immigrants.

In summarizing, we are reminded that there are significant differences between the marital relationships of first- and second-generation immigrants in the subject community. Marriage among the latter is more egalitarian, and women have achieved both status and power in the family as well as the larger community. They are no longer submissive wives threatened by their husbands. If anything, but in a very subtle way, women now "have the edge."

PARENTS AND CHILDREN

Parents in this community have one major goal: to raise children to have lives that will be significantly different from their own.[23] What one father said in response to a question dealing with his sons' future illustrates that theme very well:

You're asking me how I would feel if my sons followed in my footsteps? Are you kidding? That's the last thing I would want to happen. I mean, hey, my job is nothin'. I don't even think about what I'm doin'. I just put parts in a machine. But hell, I don't deserve any better. I never finished high school, and can't do much of anything else. But with my kids it's gonna be a different story. They're gonna stay in school and study their asses off so they can get into college and get a good job—like working in an office or even teaching school. Yeah, my kids are gonna wear suits and ties to work. And they're not gonna come home all smelly and dirty like me. No sir, you can bet on that. My wife and I are here to see to that.

Thus, we can see that family life is centered on the children and their future. Indeed, at times it is as if men and women exist not as individuals in their own right, with adult needs, wants, and desires, but as mothers and fathers whose primary responsibility is sacrificing for the sake of their children.

One reason parents think of the future almost exclusively in terms of the children is that they have little hope of bettering their own lot in life. "I ain't goin' nowhere," said a forty-one-year-old father of three. "Twenty years from now my job ain't gonna be any different. I'm stuck in this position until I retire." Men are also aware of how the larger society devalues blue-collar workers.[24] Indeed, they expect others to demean their jobs, and will not discuss what they do or the work situation until assured that others are sincerely interested. "Me?" one man said in response to my question about his job, "I just work in a factory. Nothing special. Same old thing day after day now for twenty years. But it pays the bills, so I can't complain."

Men seem especially aware of society's attitudes toward those who work with their hands when they interact with someone who is not a blue-collar worker. For example, when our TV broke down I requested help from one of the neighbor men, a drill-press operator who happened to be a self-taught, highly skilled TV repairman. I confessed my ignorance while he went about changing transistors and adjusting dials. Propped up on the set was a book he referred to every so often to make sure things were being done according to the manufacturer's specifications. Yet when I commented on how difficult his work seemed, he laughed quietly, and said:

> Yeah, I guess it seems that way. But it's not that tough, especially for someone like you, who's educated. Hell, if you put your mind to it you'd know what to do in a few minutes. Me, well, I'm pretty slow; it takes me a long time to learn this stuff. And then too, that's all I can do—fix TVs and operate a drill press.

A separate but related characteristic of men, which, as we shall see later, influences child-rearing patterns, is the feeling that it is wrong to complain about the job situation:

> Nobody owes me nothin'. If my factory closes up tomorrow and moves out of state I have nothing to complain about. They've been good to me. After all, they've let me have a job for eighteen years now. And I've been rewarded by being able to support the family. If they move I'll go and find another job. And when people see how hard I work they'll keep me on the payroll. That's all I expect; decent pay for hard work. Now it's gettin' so that the younger guys and the Black people are always asking for more and more benefits. What do they expect? Something for nothing.

"I'm just dumb," or "factory work is all I'm good for" are common expressions which tell us how men in this community see themselves and their status in society. While they seem fully aware of the existing stereotypes of Polish Americans and blue-collar workers, the fact that they are not highly valued members of society is viewed as a result of personal failings rather than social inequality.[25] Those feelings are what Richard Sennett and Jonathan Cobb have appropriately called "the hidden injuries of class."[26]

One result of feeling personally inadequate, according to those authors, is "the resolve to sacrifice for others, especially for the sake of the children, so that they might someday lead a better way of life."[27] This parental goal can have paradoxical consequences. In working-class families, as Sennett and Cobb sensitively describe, children, especially sons, are asked to take their father's life as a warning rather than as a model.[28] So, in effect, children are encouraged to become unlike their parents.[29]

How, in practice, does that work?

Perhaps the most common advice sons receive from their fathers goes something like this: "You'd better get on the ball, buddy, or you're going to end up just like me, sweating in some lousy factory just to make ends meet." Ruth Tabrah, a novelist, has captured that facet of life in a Polish-American community in the following passage, from *Pulaski Place*, when the father talks with his sons, and pleads with the youngest, Ben, not to quit high school:

Yah. I don't want either of you boys to be like me. It's all right when you're young, you're strong, then you can work like a machine and do as good as the next guy and the pay check is nice and big. You get married and get a family and first thing you know, maybe you're forty, forty-five and you're not so strong anymore and they take a little chunk out of your pay check, they put you down in a lower job. You got a education, you got a chance to work up into foreman. But like me, only to school until I was fourteen, sixth grade here to Our Lady School and then into the Bolt Works and by the time you, Steve, was fourteen and you, Benny, was just a little kid, I was already off the machines and on nights sweeping, with a pay check less than what I had the first week I started work. The same with your grandfather, it happened too. He didn't have no school at all over in the old country. Came over here when he was nineteen, and he helped build the Bolt Works. He was a strong man and he made what he thought was big wages, enough to feed the twelve of us and send us all to the sixth grade in school. By the time I go to work he is forty, he is an old man they tell him and he gets the broom to push or else maybe he wants to quit. So he's a sweeper nights too, until he die—and George Milicki, who was a laborer with him when the Bolt Works was built, he had a good education, he went right up to be foreman, and when your grandfather died this George Milicki was still making the big money. Only five years ago he retired. You remember the big wreath with the carnations he sent to your grandfather's funeral, the biggest wreath on the casket except for the one from Dom Polski. That youngest Milicki girl, the smart one, he sent her all the way through college! Something fancy she is, like a cook only smarter and the money she earns at that hospital! And his oldest son, he sent to be a dentist! Aye, Benny, I tell you that with one more year in high school to go you are a fool that you should quit now! You listen to your brother![30]

The men in this community, however, do not use the grammar or syntax of Mr. Kowalski, the father of Ben and Steve in *Pulaski Place*. Nor would they be content with their sons merely completing high school or working as a foreman. But Mr. Kowalski speaks for many working-class fathers when he says, "I don't want either of you boys to be like me."

The fact that parents want a better way of life for their children, and have resolved to sacrifice in order to provide it, is the key to understanding what it means to grow up in the subject community. Also important are parental notions of what it takes to succeed, and of how they anticipate the occupational demands that will be placed on their children. For even though mothers and fathers would like their children to become members of the professional middle class, or middle-level executives, the prevailing patterns of child-rearing are based on what parents, especially fathers, have learned about the qualities that insure success in the blue-collar world: obedience, self-control, respect for authority, and determination.

That is why child-rearing patterns are characterized by strict discipline and an emphasis on obedience. "You gotta show them who's boss," one father said, "and there's only one way to do that. Be tough—that's the way they learn respect for their elders." The need to be "tough" was a theme I heard repeatedly during interviews. Here is how one mother described what it meant in her family:

We believe in being tough right in the beginning. Spanking is good for them until they get too big. Then it doesn't hurt anymore, and you have to find other ways to punish them. You just find out out what they like to do and don't let them do it. But I'll tell you, nothin' works when they get old unless you're tough when they're young. We were, and our kids never refuse to do what they're told because they know damn well what will happen. We don't care how old they are, as long as they live under this roof they have to listen to us.

Another mother criticized a child psychologist she had seen on TV because he was too permissive:

He wants me to tell the kids *why* I want them to do one thing or another; you know, give them reasons. That's a lot of bull! When I say something those kids better jump. And if they ask why I'll tell them why. Because I'm your mother, that's why. Any more questions and they'll get a good whack on the butt, in spite of what that psychologist said.

Most mothers in the community say they prefer to discipline a child immediately rather than waiting for the father to get home from work. But what often happens is that the child is punished twice: during the day by the mother, and in the evening by the father. Thus, although mothers are primarily responsible for discipline, fathers do play a role, especially when the child has done something the parents consider a serious breach of the rules.

The strict atmosphere that prevails in the home is carried over into the classrooms of the parish school. Corporal punishment in the earlier grades is not uncommon, even though parents have recently begun to complain about teachers striking their children. Despite those grievances, physical punishment continues to exist and is indeed encouraged by some parents.

Parents also control their children by rewarding behavior considered to be desirable. Gans's description of how the reward and punishment method operated among the Italian-American families in the West End of Boston applies to this community as well:

There is a continuous barrage of prohibitions and threats, intertwined with words and deeds of reward and affection. But the torrents of threats and cajolery neither impinge on the feelings of parental affection, nor are meant as signs of rejection. As one mother explained to her child, "We hit you because we love you." People believe that discipline is needed constantly to keep the child in line with and respectful of adult rules, and that without it he would run amok.[31]

When you ask parents to describe the ideal child, one behavioral characteristic appears preeminent: obedience. "They *must* listen to us," one wife said as her husband nodded in agreement. "They *must* realize that we are the bosses. If the kids do what we say they will never be punished." Another father said:

> A kid who obeys his parents is a good kid. And he's gotta listen to his teachers, too, no questions asked. We are the ones who know best, because we are the adults. Folks who think you gotta dialogue with kids or cater to their every whim will have spoiled brats. What raising kids is all about is getting them to obey, to listen to what you say, to do what you say they should do.

Studies of middle-class families show that strict discipline and obedience are ranked lower in importance compared to parental expectations in working-class homes.[32] And some observers, after examining those findings, conclude that parents from the working class are insensitive if not authoritarian. But it is important to analyze child-rearing patterns from the parents' point of view.

For example, Robert A. LeVine, in discussing societies that value the childhood development of compliance, says, "it seems clear that obedience is something parents want *for* their children not simply *from* them."[33] Why? Because mothers and fathers "are anticipating the occupational demands their children will face, as Kohn has argued for the Western working classes."[34] LeVine goes on to show the necessity of considering the relationship between child-rearing patterns and economic status. His comments deserve our attention:

> The present interpretation is somewhat different from Kohn's however, because I believe that parental values are more constrained and influenced by economic factors when economic survival is in greater jeopardy. While Kohn sees middle-class as well as working-class parental values equally influenced by occupational roles, I argue that insofar as the environment of working-class people is more hazardous and the resources scarcer, their child-rearing con-

ceptions should be more rigidly dominated by considerations of the child's future economic well-being. In an economic environment of stable affluence, parents can evolve child-rearing philosophies and fashions that are less tightly coupled to the hazards of economic failure; they are relatively free to pursue in their child-rearing a wide variety of cultural and personal goals beyond those dictated by sheer material survival. From this point of view, the differences in child-rearing values between Western working-class and middle-class parents may represent differences in their subjective economic security that in turn reflect the actual material positions to which they have become adapted.[35]

So let us take care not to engage in "blaming the victim," in criticizing working-class parents for being strict and for emphasizing the development of obedience in their children. For parental values are forged from experience, from economic insecurity and uncertainty, from what it takes to succeed working day after day, hour after hour, on the line, never complaining, always following the boss's orders—from being obedient.

Yet the patterns of child-rearing we discussed do have serious limitations. For what children learn does not prepare them for the way of life they experience outside the shelter of an urban Polish-American community, or the blue-collar world. Indeed, there are discontinuities between growing up in that culture and encountering the larger society.[36]

The submissive, obedient, and cautious child who feels comfortable in his family, parish, neighborhood is ill-at-ease as a young adult on a college campus or in a job that requires a capacity for independent thought and self-direction.[37] Young adults have problems expressing themselves and fear people in positions of authority, much as they feared their parents and teachers. And like their fathers, they have problems in a competitive environment and feel uncomfortable being aggressive. So often they assume a defensive posture and refuse to "rock the boat" or complain for fear of being fired or failing in school.[38]

Those, then, are some of the more important consequences of a child-rearing approach based on the use of parental power. While they reflect the problems involved in attempting to cross the cultural barrier between a Polish-American community and the outside world, we must remember that that is what parents want for their children. The fact that the majority of children in this community do not go on to college or lead lives significantly different from their parents in no way indicates a lack of desire or ability.[39] Rather, it is strong evidence of a lack of opportunity and the continued existence of a way of life culturally distinct from the larger society.[40] Many young adults realize just how different that life is, and are frightened by the prospect of not being able to cope with change.

Parents, too, are ambivalent. They want their children to succeed, to have a "better way of life," to leave the community. But seeing children out on their own, away from home, is difficult, especially for mothers. In the TV series entitled "Six American Families," a working-class Polish-American family was featured. One of the most poignant moments of the show was when the eldest son, Gary, an aspiring actor, talked about his mother:

> She turns out good people. But she harms them too because she raises children in one world and you have to live in another one. You have to raise kids today and then let them go at the right time so they can go out and experiment in their own. Because, after a while, if you keep the apron strings too tight, it begins to hurt.[41]

Sacrificing for the sake of the children thus entails a tremendous risk on the part of parents. For if the children are unsuccessful in achieving a "better way of life" their parents feel betrayed. "It just goes to show you how ungrateful kids can be," said one father. "You work your ass off for years so the kid can get a college education and what does he do? He quits school to work in a factory, that's what. So what's the point of sacrificing?"

The point of sacrificing, as we have already mentioned, is so that children will become unlike their parents. What that means, unfortunately, is that some parents who succeed in raising children to be successful in the outside world also feel betrayed, though they feel that for very different reasons. "Our son thinks he's too good for us now that he's gone to college, got himself a high-paying job, and bought a big house in the suburbs," complained one mother. "He uses big words and thinks we're old-fashioned. That's what we get for buying him books and putting him through school."

The theme of sacrifice, then, does not always guarantee that parents will be satisfied in later life. Indeed, this section of the study has shown that the results may be painful, for parents and children alike.

That pain, however, is caused by societal attitudes toward ethnicity and social class. For the sons and daughters of immigrants have been required to reject their cultural heritage in order to be successful in the larger society. And doing just that has made them ambivalent about their parents' way of life. I recall my first few weeks in Detroit, when I was talking with many Polish Americans from all walks of life about my plans to study "the old neighborhood." Below are some of the reactions of third- and fourth-generation Poles I encountered, some of whom were professionals, one a priest, all now suburbanites:

"You mean you came back to Detroit *just* to study Polish Americans?"

"You mean you really want to live in the 'old neighborhood?' "

"So you're moving into Archie Bunker land, eh? And after all those years in graduate school. What a pity!"[42]

Now I'm not saying that everyone responded that way, nor that all children are ambivalent when it comes to the attitudes and values of their parents. But the problem does exist, and we need to recognize that it stems from the fact that class change, especially when we consider the ethnic factor, can be "a viciously destructive process."[43]

I remember, too, when I first moved into the neighborhood, several residents were surprised. "Someone with your education? You're going to live here?" one woman said. "Why, you *belong* in Warren or Sterling Heights." Others reacted in similar fashion, and somehow, very subtly of course, I was viewed as a failure for choosing to live where I did.

No, there is nothing wrong with hard work and sacrifice. Indeed, that is the only way immigrants managed to earn a decent living, to stay out of debt and provide for their children, to survive. But there is something quite wrong with a society that says who you are is based on what you do for a living, that uses the color of a man's collar as a measure of his intelligence, a society that leads parents to sacrifice, to live vicariously through their children be-

cause they themselves don't count. Many mothers and fathers
sacrifice for their children, but as Sennett and Cobb remind us,
those from the middle class have more chance of "sacrificing successfully."[44] And less fear of being betrayed. For they need not tell
their children, "Don't be like us."

The Parish 5

In an earlier chapter we found that the parish was instrumental in establishing and maintaining the urban Polish-American community that serves as the focus of this study. Our discussion dealt primarily with how the parish, by performing both social and religious functions, provided the framework for what the sociologist Raymond Breton has termed an "institutionally complete community."[1] In the pages that follow, however, there is a shift in emphasis: I shall describe and analyze selected dimensions of parish life rather than depict St. Thaddeus as the source of social organization for the wider community.

What can we learn of the life style, patterns of behavior, and values of working-class Polish Americans by examining parish life? That is the underlying question of the present chapter. From the beginning, we have emphasized that the lives of people in the subject community revolve around three separate yet related spheres: the family, the parish, and the neighborhood. From our discussion of family life we now understand a great deal about the residents. That notwithstanding, more of their way of life will continue to unfold as we consider the relationship between the pastor and his parishioners, as well as the religious, organizational, social, educational, and cultural scope of St. Thaddeus.

THE PASTOR

The history of any Catholic parish is greatly influenced by the personality, style, and interests of its pastors. And that is all the more true with regard to Polish-American parishes, for the role of a pastor as an "all-powerful" leader in Poland has to some extent

87

been retained here in America. Indeed, until recently, pastors of Polish extraction have been regarded with veneration and even awe. That is not to imply, however, an immunity to criticism. In fact, quite the opposite is true: evaluating the pastor is a favorite topic of conversation among Detroit's Polonia. And the query "Who's your pastor?" is certain to encourage lively banter, perhaps even an argument.

Pastors evoke strong feelings because they are more than just spiritual leaders. People not only view them as heads of communities but as intermediaries with the larger society. And, more important, pastors are symbolic figures. They provide the means through which a community expresses its sense of unity and individuality. For what distinguishes one Polish-American community from another is the fact they are identified with different pastors. So while the geographic location of parishes is significant in differentiating Polish settlements, it is the pastors who give symbolic meaning to those differences, who serve to establish the basis for community in the psychological sense of the word, and who influence the ethos of their respective groups.

Fr. Sylvester Kaminski, the first pastor of St. Thaddeus parish, is a case in point. Recently retired after more than forty years as pastor, Fr. Kaminski still remains active, saying mass on Sundays and participating in social events and organizational activities. Referred to as a living legend by some, the elderly priest will always be remembered: a bust of him, commissioned by parishioners, adorns the foyer of the activities building, insuring that. Not many pastors are so honored.

Yet there are two points of view regarding Fr. Kaminski. While some parishioners admire his administrative skill in founding the parish and overseeing the construction of an impressive complex of buildings, others complain that he was constructing monuments to himself, and that he was a "tightwad."

Those who respect and praise the retired pastor tell of how he "dug in" and served as the general contractor when the cost estimates for erecting the new church ran too high. They mention how he painted and did maintenance work around the parish, stressing that most Polish pastors feel such work is beneath them. It was Fr. Kaminski, his supporters claim, who got people together to build the first wooden church, along with help from a contractor. It was he, almost single-handedly, who erected a grotto on the parish grounds in honor of Our Lady of Częstochowa, the patron saint of Poland. And it was he, people say, who nurtured the growth of the parish from two hundred families in 1925 to four hundred and fifty in 1940, and from eight hundred in 1948 to twelve hundred and fifty in 1954.[2] Finally, the fact that St. Thaddeus has not experienced a significant decline in parishioners during the early 1970s, as have many other urban parishes, is due primarily to the leadership of Fr. Kaminski, his admirers boast.

The dissenters argue that the first pastor was too concerned with building things and collecting the necessary monies. They are quick to mention their resentment toward his so-called "home visits," when it was difficult to turn down the priest's request for a donation. Also unpopular was the elderly pastor's habit of personally collecting contributions during Sunday mass. "That should have been done by the ushers," reported one long-time parishioner. "But when Fr. Kaminski did it we felt pressured. How could you look him in the eye without putting a few bucks in the basket?" People reacted similarly to the manner in which the retired priest had presented his annual report to the parishioners: every January, from the pulpit, Fr. Kaminski would read a carefully prepared list, detailing the total amount of money donated by each parishioner during the preceding year. One of the older church members recalled:

> He pressured us—and it was difficult and embarrassing if you hadn't shelled out the money. Because when he would get up in that pulpit and start reading names everyone in the parish would know how much you gave. So we gave. Even when we couldn't afford it!

Some members of parish organizations reacted strongly to the founding pastor's attempts to keep expenses to the minimum. A member of the Dad's Club explained:

> So what if he built a nice gymnasium? What good is it if he's gonna shut off the lights during a basketball game? And that's just what he did. Would you believe that the guy walked across the gym floor right in the middle of a ball game and shut off the lights? He said

we didn't need lights because the game was in the afternoon, and it was still light outside. But that was pure bull; the players couldn't see each other, and they sure as hell couldn't see the basket. But that's what he did. And it really made me mad, because it was our money he was trying to save.

Others complain that Fr. Kaminski made all the important decisions, that he was like a very strict father who treated his parishioners like children, very young children. "We were afraid of him," a former president of one of the women's organizations remarked, "and I think he wanted it that way." But despite the grumbling, Fr. Kaminski *was* the pastor. And when he led, people followed.

The new pastor, Fr. Edward Bulakowski, is different from Fr. Kaminski. Yet he too, perhaps like all leaders, is loved by some and hated by others.

His supporters say he "opened up" the parish meeting rooms and the gymnasium. They argue that things are more alive now, that activities and events have increased, that the gymnasium is in use almost every day and evening—with all the lights on. Fr. Bulakowski is praised for treating parishioners like "adults," for being accessible and having the capacity to listen. "If we want something we just go in and see him," said one member of the Madonna Guild. "There's no hassling about pennies anymore. He's real nice, and gives us what we ask for."

On the other hand, many parishioners were upset when they learned that Fr. Bulakowski was slated to become their new pastor. The problem was a complex one. To begin with, Polish Americans in Detroit have always felt discriminated against by the local church hierarchy. And under John Cardinal Dearden, those feelings have continued, based now on the argument that he is responsive to the needs of Blacks in the city but unsympathetic to the problems of working-class Polish-American communities.[3] Then into the picture steps Fr. Bulakowski, a priest whose last assignment was serving a Black parish in the inner city, a man who one Polish American described as "the Polish priest who spends his time working with Blacks when he should be helping his own people."

And so, the people of St. Thaddeus were apprehensive about Fr. Bulakowski. "Why, at first we thought he was an 'agent' of

Cardinal Dearden," one elderly woman told me. "We were sure he was going to say we should all move, and turn over our neighborhood to Black folks." Then to further complicate matters, there was even a rumor that the new pastor would remove from the church all the statues of white saints and replace them with Black ones. As incredible as those rumors might seem to outsiders, people's fears were real. So Fr. Bulakowski was forced to deal with them.

At a large community meeting, called by parishioners, the articulate priest answered questions. No, he assured them, the church would remain the same. The statues would stay, and there would be no Black saints. Parish members were also relieved to learn that the new pastor thought Polish-American communities were wonderful, that members of an ethnic group had the right to live together if they chose. Yet the questions persisted. "Are you acting under directions from the cardinal?" Fr. Bulakowski was asked. "And what do you think of the archdiocese taxing the Poles to give money to the Blacks?" was another query. Once the priest dealt with those matters satisfactorily he began to win the people's confidence. But the process has been a slow one, and it remains unfinished. Meanwhile, parishioners now evaluate Fr. Bulakowski on his own strengths and weaknesses as an administrator and spiritual leader, not as a representative of the archdiocese. For example, Dad's Club members wish he would attend more meetings, while others complain that he hasn't done enough to stop the neighborhood's rising crime rate. Generally speaking, then, the new pastor will be remembered for what he does, or does not, accomplish during the years ahead.

RELIGION, TRADITION, AND CHANGE

Sophie Maliszewski was in tears. We had just been to a meeting at which changes in the church were discussed. She was upset by what the speaker for the evening, a young theologian, had said: that purgatory was not a place, but a *symbol* of the process of temporal punishment.[4] Sophie and I talked as we made our way toward our respective homes. "I don't understand it," said the fifty-two-year-old grandmother,

How can they say that after all these years? I've been praying for my mother and father every day—they always told us to pray for the "poor souls in purgatory" so that someday they could get into heaven. Now they make it seem that I was wasting my time. But what really bothers me is I worry about my parents. My God! If there's no purgatory, where are they?

Sophie Maliszewski is typical of the second-generation adults who belong to St. Thaddeus. They learned their catechism well, perhaps *too well*, some of the younger generation say. The church and its priests were never questioned; nor were the rules and regulations that had to be followed in order to remain "in a state of grace," to earn the right to enter heaven after death. Presently, with the Catholic church changing rapidly in response to Vatican II and Pope John, Sophie Maliszewski's generation feels threatened and a little lost or betrayed.

For no longer is it considered appropriate to say the rosary at mass or follow along quietly in the Latin missal. Now people are asked to participate, either in Polish or English. They are also asked to shake hands with each other before Holy Communion and say, "Peace be with you," to involve them in the "Kiss of Peace." Folk music has replaced Latin hymns, and the younger people have suddenly become important participants in services once devoted primarily to serving the needs of adults. Men and women who grew up listening to a choir led by an unobtrusive organist now see and hear three teenagers who stand in the sacristy strumming guitars, singing folk melodies. The parishioners of St. Thaddeus have been asked to change the very way they worship. Their reactions to those changes provide insights into the meaning of religion in the lives of working-class Polish Americans.

John Krajewski, a forty-two-year-old tool and die worker and father of four, discusses how he and his wife feel about the "new Catholic church":

It's ridiculous. We don't feel holy when we go to church, anymore. It's too loud to say the rosary and they tell us it don't do no good to use the missals we paid good money for. So what the hell do we do? You ain't gonna catch the wife and I singing those songs from TV and radio. Not in church. Why, it's sacrilegious. Like shaking hands with the person next to you, and holding the Communion host in your hands. Hell, when we were kids they told us our fingers would fall off if we touched the host; and that we were committing a sin if we tried to chew it. Now everything is different. But we don't feel comfortable. And somehow it just don't seem right, if you know what I mean.

Men like John Krajewski do have an option: they may attend a High Mass said in Polish, or a Low Mass celebrated by Fr. Kaminski in both Latin and Polish. But John's children prefer the other masses. So he and his wife "sacrifice," as they put it. For attending church with the entire family is considered an important tradition.

All of the adult men and women interviewed, and the many others I came to know, attended Sunday mass regularly. And most felt it was necessary to go to confession if they missed, even if the cause was beyond their control. "It's a good idea to report you couldn't make it to mass," said Peter Ogonowicz, "even if you had to work. You gotta 'keep the slate clean,' because you can't take the chance of getting in an accident or something like that with a mortal sin on your soul."

Thus, fear of eternal damnation has been one of the motivating forces behind their church attendance and adherence to the rules of the Roman Catholic religion. The extent to which that motive pervades the religious behavior and general attitudes of second-, and to a lesser extent, third-generation parishioners is evident, as well, from how parents reacted to the possibility their children might receive First Holy Communion without having gone to confession. The official archdiocesan position was children of seven were incapable of committing a mortal sin, thus confession was not a prerequisite to receiving First Communion.[5]

Yet the majority of parents who had assembled to hear that point of view explained were horrified by what they learned. "How can you go to communion without going to confession?" a mother of four asked, "even if you are only seven years old." Another woman voiced a separate but related concern: "If we do what the archdiocese suggests the kids won't be afraid of doing the wrong thing; they have to learn to be afraid when they're young, or when they grow up they'll become 'fallen-away Catholics' and rotten people."

While such an approach to religion insures strong guilt feelings

if a rule is broken—by children or adults—it also provides a sense
of security if one believes he or she is living up to the precepts of
the church. Furthermore, since the sacrament of confession is
available to those who err, there is a built-in mechanism for
"clearing the slate," as one informant put it.

People of St. Thaddeus appear to be dissatisfied with the frequency and intensity of their participation in religious activities,
especially the women. A theme I heard repeatedly during interviews
and conversations was the desire to become "a better Catholic."

"Attending Sunday Mass and receiving the sacraments just isn't
enough," a middle-aged woman said. "I should be attending daily
mass, but I just don't have the time."

Here in the community women are more devout than the men,
but Polish-American males in no way resemble the stereotype of
Latin men who view religion—or going to mass—as a purely femi-
nine concern. The number of adult males in St. Thaddeus who
receive communion each Sunday is high. Yet being a "good Catholic" for husbands and fathers involves other kinds of behavior,
especially toward one's wife and family. Thus, while men frequently joke about their own sexual desires toward "other women,"
they also express a reluctance to become involved in extramarital
affairs or brief liaisons. "I just couldn't live with myself if I fooled
around with another woman," said a thirty-five-year-old known for
his youthful good looks and charming manner,

> because committing adultery is breaking one of the command-
> ments, and even with confession I could never forgive myself for
> such a serious sin. And, hell, I could never look my wife straight in
> the eye again without feeling guilty. The kids too. How could I be a
> good father if I fooled around with another woman? No way, not
> me, I'm a Catholic, and that means being a faithful husband and a
> good father.

So, although talking about sex is common, men who remain
faithful to their wives is the norm.

In an earlier chapter we mentioned that both men and women
feel that the Catholic church should adopt a more liberal position
on divorce; the same is true with regard to birth control. But
people are careful to point out that what they believe the rules
ought to be does not necessarily govern their own behavior. Thus,

divorce and the pill are acceptable for other couples, not in their own family. Yet it is significant to note that parishioners are questioning church policy in those two areas.

Nevertheless, archdiocesan attempts to promote a re-examination of traditional religious beliefs and practices, to suggest that being a "good Christian" is based more on "putting Christianity into practice," and less on fear or such traditional criteria as attending Sunday mass and receiving the sacraments, were relatively unsuccessful. For as we suggested earlier, to raise questions on what one was taught by nuns and priests was viewed as sinful if not sacrilegious. In short, you lived your faith; you didn't ask why. Now, even if the cardinal said it was time to change, somehow it didn't seem right. And that is why a series of archdiocesan-sponsored discussion groups designed to exchange ideas about Catholicism in the 1970s at the parish level were poorly attended.[6] While it is true that working-class Polish Americans felt uncomfortable in small seminar-type groups, their lack of interest and minimal participation were due more to a rejection of what was being discussed than to dissatisfaction with the style or tone of the meetings.

There has been a similar response to parish-based programs initiated by the Christian Education Commission, a small group of individuals also concerned with discussing contemporary Christianity. As one of the organizers of that group put it, "We can get people to come to a card party or bingo, but when we sponsor anything having to do with discussing religion, or rather, how we approach our religion, forget it; they just won't come, even when we serve coffee and cake afterwards."

Thus the religious dimension of parish life is characterized by strict adherence to the traditional rules of the church, and the reluctance to accept change. The symbols and rituals that once provided a sense of comfort and security—a support system, if you will—are no longer the same. Perhaps they have been altered too quickly in light of what the anthropologist Clifford Geertz tells us about their role:

> Sacred symbols function to synthesize a people's ethos—the tone, character, and quality of their life, its moral and aesthetic style and mood—the picture they have of the way things in actuality are, their most comprehensive idea of order.[7]

Reactions have been different among the younger generation. Despite parents' attempts to rear children to share their beliefs and attitudes, those sons and daughters have begun to lose interest in the church, and to question its value and relevance. Thus, school children rebel at being forced to attend mass during the week, ridiculing their parents' unquestioning approach to religion. In a discussion on the church, my eighth-grade students at the parish school concluded that "going to church has absolutely nothing to do with being a good person, but it sure is helpful if you want to meet friends and find out what's happening." Nevertheless, grade-school and high-school students do attend mass regularly; partly because they are forced to by their parents, and partly because they enjoy mingling with their friends. But, in general, the younger generation is less fearful of incurring God's wrath and more inclined to view religion as a "take it or leave it" proposition.

The relationship between ethnicity—in terms of national origin—and religion is the final subject for discussion in this section of the present chapter. In a consideration of "The Cultures of Catholicism," Harold Abramson draws upon H. Richard Niebuhr to explain that relationship:

> The Catholicism of Mediterranean countries, as well as of Ireland, is rooted not so much in the ethnic character of the peoples as in historical conditions, which, however influenced by ethnic factors, have been subject also to other and more decisive influences . . . . Perhaps religion is as often responsible for ethnic character as the latter is responsible for the faith.[8]

And, in an attempt to focus in on the Irish, the same problem is posed in the following statement by Thomas N. Brown:

> Perhaps the greatest difficulty which confronts the historian of the Irish is that of differentiating between the specifically Irish and specifically Catholic aspects of their lives. They have emerged into the modern world from a past in which Catholicism had played a stronger role than among any other people of Western Europe.[9]

So we cannot expect to separate what is Catholic and what is Polish-American about the behavior and values of Americans of Polish extraction. But it is possible to offer observations on how the Church's teachings affect their day-to-day life.

Their early religious instruction has instilled in them a fear of sin, especially mortal sin. Moreover, many second-generation working-class Polish Americans seem to feel that punishment or some evil will befall them if they don't follow the rules, not just the rules of the church, but most rules that apply to them as workers, students, citizens, and so on. "Don't rock the boat, don't complain, just follow the rules" were the strategies for success that I repeatedly heard.

The church teaches that it is possible—indeed necessary—to become a "better Catholic": to commit fewer sins, to act as a Christian "should" act, to think less of one's self and more of others. Yet I observed that people were quick to judge themselves "selfish" if they didn't "sacrifice," or weren't satisfied with their performance on the job because they hadn't worked "hard enough." An inordinate striving for perfection in the way the home was to be maintained or at the workplace was common.

Doubtless, those characteristics are a combination of history, religion, national origin, and social class. And, my observations should be considered as hypotheses to be tested through further studies. But certainly we have here a beginning to understanding the "cultures of Catholicism."

THE ORGANIZATIONS

The organizational dimension of parish life is a rich source of data on the lives of Polish Americans. With fifteen organizations for men, women, and children, as well as the events and activities they sponsor, this subject could well be the focus of a separate study. But our purposes will be adequately served by describing and analyzing two of the major organizations, the Dad's Club and the Madonna Guild.[10]

The Dad's Club

The Dad's Club is the most important men's organization in St. Thaddeus, though not to hear the members of the Usher's Club tell it, for competition among parish societies (or clubs, as they are more commonly called) is fierce, with loyalties contributing to one's sense of identity and social status. With nearly seventy-five members, the Dad's Club is the largest men's association. And, through financially supporting the athletic program of the school and maintaining the gymnasium and parish meeting rooms, it does make a significant contribution to the total community. In evaluating the club's role we should also mention it assumes major responsibility for running a weekly bingo game that attracts hundreds of patrons and brings in a relatively large sum of money on an annual basis. Those funds are used for the activities mentioned above, but they also support the school kindergarten and other worthwhile parish activities.

Although the club's membership is officially listed at seventy-two, we should point out that only forty men are considered "members in good standing." The rest have failed to pay their annual dues of three dollars, and are a constant source of embarrassment to the association. Indeed, each monthly meeting includes a heated discussion of the problem; the solution, say most regulars, is to prevent those who don't pay dues from attending the club's social functions. As the president put it, "The guys who want to belong just so they can attend the Christmas party will have to pay up first, and do some work at the bingo parties. They are not going to sit on their asses all year round, then say they forgot about the dues, and expect to have fun with all of us who have worked and paid our money."

Those who are active participants in the club are easily identified; they wear dark blue nylon jackets with a contrasting red and white patch sewn on the front left side. The words "St. Thaddeus Dad's Club" are boldly printed on the patch and, just below, the member's name is lettered in white thread. It is considered an honor to have such a jacket, for they are awarded only after a man has earned a required number of points through participating in club activities. In addition to identifying someone as a member in good standing, a jacket provides men with a feeling of pride, serving as a symbol of their worth outside the immediate community.

While most current members joined the club when their children were students in the parish school, many continue to belong long after their sons and daughters have entered high school or college or have begun working. And that is because they enjoy attending meetings and feel committed to working for the good of the parish. Besides, for some, the Dad's Club is their only source of recreation and leisure outside the home.

Perhaps the best way to provide a picture of the club and its members is to describe a typical monthly meeting. The following description is based on my written observations of sixteen such gatherings.

Dad's Club meetings are held in a cafeteria located in the rear of the activities building, a structure that also includes a fairly large gymnasium with showers and locker rooms for boys and girls. The cafeteria and gym are separated by a sliding plastic partition so that both may be used at the same time.

For meetings the cafeteria is arranged with one long table facing four or five others lined up parallel to one another, each with ten metal chairs, five to a side. The front table is for the officers: the president, vice-president, recording secretary, financial secretary, and treasurer. A small statue of St. John Bosco, the patron saint of youth and, thus, the club, is placed in the middle of the table, directly in front of the president. Next to the statue is a wooden gavel used to call the meeting to order and quiet the membership when necessary. The name of the club's first president is inscribed on the gavel, along with the founding date of the organization.

The meeting is scheduled to begin at 7:30 P.M. Still, the officers arrive a half-hour early to discuss the agenda. While they talk, members begin filtering in. They sit wherever a chair is available, which is very different from the pattern of seating at women's organizations, as described later in this chapter.

Club members range in age from thirty-five to fifty-five, though most are over forty. They dress in a variety of styles, from bell-bottoms and Arnold Palmer sweaters to work pants and sport shirts. Yet their hands—hard, heavily calloused—tell the story. You realize that these are men whose hands are the means to their living, which also means being physically active, not sitting behind a desk or standing behind a podium. You also become aware why so few of the club members are overweight, why most of them are trim and well-built. And then you listen again.

While waiting for the meeting to begin these men converse on various topics, but mostly sports, especially if their sons and daughters play on parish teams. Their language is peppered generously with expletives, which seems incongruous with the way the meeting begins. My field notes from one of the first gatherings I attended illustrate what I mean:

> As I sat down on one of the metal chairs I overheard a conversation between two men sitting next to me. One was saying, " . . . and I told that goddam coach that if he didn't start letting my son play I'd raise so much hell. . . . " But before the member could complete his sentence the club president was banging his gavel and starting the Our Father. All the men stopped talking, stood up, folded their hands, and began to pray as they reverently bowed their heads. That was the start of the meeting.

It was conducted according to parliamentary procedure. A sergeant at arms (elected along with the rest of the officers) is supposed to maintain order but is rarely called upon since the president prefers to use the gavel, precluding more stringent measures. Generally, the meetings are more closely structured than most I have attended at a federal agency or educational institution. Yet at times members will speak out while an officer is delivering a report or a member is raising a question. Indeed, one Dad has a reputation for comments like "you don't know what you're talking about." But he is usually silenced quickly by the president with a polite but firm "you're outta order."

An agenda is followed carefully, of which the roll call of the officers is the first order of business. And that is followed by the minutes of the last meeting, the financial secretary's report and the treasurer's accounting of funds received and dispersed. The latter is perhaps of most interest, for the men hear the tangible results of their efforts to assist the children of the parish.

Included in the treasurer's report is a statement of income from bingo and amounts spent on various items: e.g., coaches' salaries, uniforms for the school teams, entry fees for tournaments, and health insurance for the players. Here, at least one of the members is sure to complain about the large sums being spent on the school athletic program. He is usually shouted down by the rest of the group. "Knock it off," the men will say, "don't you know this is for the kids? What are we here for if we can't help them out?"

Also, many Dads are experts in parliamentary procedure, because of their involvement in union meetings at work, and they react strongly to those who speak "out of order." Indeed, at times very complicated discussions ensue on motions already on the floor—on who has the right to talk, and what it takes to pass or amend the motion.

Once the treasurer's report is read and approved, "unfinished business" is next, followed then by "new business," an agenda item that provides the observer with a wealth of information on the Dad's Club, its members, and the way of life in this community.

For instance, one of the issues during the last few months of this study was a motion to purchase window curtains for the gym, so the men could show movies to parish youngsters on Saturday mornings. It was heartily approved, as are most suggestions that involve providing the children with opportunities for recreation and leisure. In fact, the most prevalent cause for arguments at a Dad's Club meeting is a motion to spend money on themselves—for an evening at the ballpark or racetrack—instead of on the youngsters. It seems, therefore, that an overriding concern for the kids of the parish is one of the defining characteristics of the club.

In that regard it is interesting to note that one of the major events in the social life of the parish—and perhaps the most popular—is the Dad's Club Christmas party. A full dinner is served to members and their families, free drinks are provided, and a small orchestra plays until after midnight. But more significantly, it is an evening dedicated to the children. They each receive a gift from Santa Claus, and are allowed to stay up later than usual. The occasion is a festive one: the dance floor is crowded with beaming youngsters, from toddlers to teenagers, who join hands with the adults to sing and dance for an evening of joy. And Dad's Club members do not concern themselves with a cost of over a thousand dollars. What really matters is that the kids and, to a lesser extent, their parents have a good time.

In addition to learning how the Dad's Club reinforces the emphasis on the lives of children in this community, it is also possible to discern from their meetings their attitudes toward work, and how they view women, subjects that were previously addressed in the chapter on the family. For example, an excerpt from my notes on "new business" deals with a discussion of the summer picnic, but it reveals much more:

One member suggested that the picnic be held on a Saturday. Another said that was impossible, because some men work then. "Are you kidding?" asked a third. "Just how many of us are lucky enough to work overtime, especially during the summer?" Finally, it was decided to table the issue until May, when the members would have a better idea of their work schedules.

With regard to coordinating and organizing the picnic, it was suggested that the Dad's Club invite the Madonna Guild to participate in the event. "Maybe if we invite the women to come they'll handle all the arrangements," said one man half-jokingly. "You know how efficient those women are," he continued. "Why, if they take it over we can just sit back and have a good time."

Once "new business" has been dispensed with there are committee reports and "remarks for the good of the club." Then the session closes with a prayer, after which the officers and members say, "St. John Bosco, pray for us." And then the social hour begins.

Men gather in small groups of two or three to drink beer and eat pizza or sandwiches provided by the club. They speak mostly of sports, the issues raised at the meeting, and other parish affairs. Work, politics, or family life are topics that receive very little attention. For some the high point of the evening is the opportunity to play pinochle or poker; several games start immediately after the final prayer but rarely last very long, since most of the men leave before midnight.

The Madonna Guild

The Madonna Guild is an organization founded in 1949 "to promote sociability among young married women of the parish, to stimulate religious interest, and to work for the welfare of the school children," according to its by-laws. Currently the club has just over a hundred members, more than 75 percent of whom are considered "active." As mentioned earlier, this organization is considered the most important one in the parish. Its officers are highly respected leaders in the community, and the club's activities are carefully planned, well-attended, and extremely important as far as the social life of the parish is concerned. The Madonna Guild has achieved its prominent position primarily because it is the main club for women, whose leadership role in the community has already been discussed.

The flow of information at its monthly meetings and the relationships formed through the association represent one of the keys to understanding the subject community. For the members maintain linkages among the nuclear families by gathering information at meetings and then passing it on to neighbors and friends—individuals who do not belong to the club. It is in that way the network of families stay in touch with one another and learn of parish events, activities, and personalities. Indeed, it is how the community is maintained.

To provide readers with an idea of just how the Madonna Guild functions, and what its members are like, we will utilize the same approach as was taken with the Dad's Club. But here I will draw on my wife's observations, for she was a member of the organization.

Meetings are held the second Monday of every month, at which sixty-five to eighty women are present. The setting is similar to that of a Dad's Club gathering, except a statue of the Blessed Virgin replaces that of St. John Bosco. But unlike the men, it is of crucial importance that women come early. For them seating arrangements are critical; when filled, the tables separate into cliques, groups of women who are on "good terms with one another." And if a member is late, and if her friends have not reserved a space, she might be forced to sit with another group, perhaps even directly across from someone with whom she is on "bad terms." So most, in order to avoid just that, arrive a half-hour early.

The women range in age from thirty to seventy, although the majority are between thirty-five and fifty-five. Most wear pantsuits, but some, usually the officers, wear dresses. All are carefully coiffed and neatly attired, a large number of them having been to the hairdresser before the meeting.

The proceedings begin with a decade of the rosary, usually led by the pastor. Throughout the remainder of the session members carry on quiet conversations. Some are devoted to gossip, while others deal with issues on the agenda. And the president's gavel is used not infrequently.

While members will talk with one another about the pros and

cons of an issue on the floor, only rarely will someone publicly question what seems like a decision or, for that matter, an officer's report. For those who do might well become the objects of discussion among the many cliques, quite apart from finding it difficult to garner support from others who might share their point of view.

Nor is it an easy task to find women who are willing to run for office. It seems that anyone who accepts a leadership position is considered to have "placed herself on a pedestal" and, thus, is open to criticism. So while the majority of members complain about "the clique that runs the club," few are eager to become officers.

Parliamentary procedure is followed at all meetings, of which the typical agenda includes the minutes of the last meeting, the treasurer's report and old and new business. In the meeting chosen to be reported on here, the treasurer announced that the club had recently purchased drapes and furniture for the faculty lounge of the grade school, and presented the pastor and his assistants with small Christmas gifts.

The committee whose job it is to comfort the sick told of its visits to members who were hospitalized, answering questions regarding such. As usual, those at the meeting asked for detailed explanations and received complete reports of, for example, the operation performed, why it was necessary, and how the patient was recuperating. Whether those visited would have appreciated the disclosures cannot be known; nevertheless, everyone present was interested in learning as much as possible about the patient, her problem, and her progress.

A very exciting part of the meeting was a discussion on the coming events to be sponsored by the club. An evening at a local nightclub, complete with dinner and drinks, was planned for the next month—and with a portion of the expenses covered by the group. And that "ladies' night out" did not include the husbands. Nor did the activity for the following month: a trip to the movies, by chartered bus, to see *Fiddler on the Roof*.

Next on the agenda was a reminder dealing with the procedures for handling the "Traveling Madonna," which is a richly decorated statue, about two feet tall, of the Blessed Virgin. It is so named because each member, in alphabetical order, has the right to keep the statue for two weeks. It comes in a specially made case to prevent breakage, is accompanied by a red votive light, and is usually placed in a prominent position in the home. Members consider it a great honor to have the Madonna in their possession, and very reverently—and perhaps a bit reluctantly—they deliver it to whoever is next on the list.

The club sponsors between ten and fifteen social events a year, some only for women, such as the Mother's Day dinner or various "Nights Out," besides others like the Mardi Gras Dance for husbands and wives. At this meeting the latter was spoken about, and a committee was appointed to hire cooks, arrange for a good band, and see that the gymnasium was properly decorated. Members were encouraged to sell tickets to their friends and relatives to insure a successful evening—judged by how much money is earned and if the people attending have a good time. Those vested with the responsibility for the Mardi Gras work on it many months in advance, and everything must be done well, if not perfectly. People of St. Thaddeus expect as much from the Madonna Guild, and they will not be disappointed.

After a meeting the members play several games of bingo and have a snack prepared by the refreshment committee. Small groups of women take turns at that, and it is viewed as an opportunity to demonstrate their culinary skills. The evening is usually over by ten o'clock, and members leave in twos and threes for fear of being mugged.

In summary, while the Madonna Guild has both social and religious functions, it should be clear that the former is more important.

SOCIAL LIFE

Music, a gaily decorated gymnasium, good food, drink, and people—those are the ingredients of a successful social event at St. Thaddeus. But a closer look will show how they all fit together.

There are nearly ten evenings during the year when husbands and wives, as well as younger unmarrieds in their late teens and early twenties, get together in a large group to enjoy themselves. All such occasions are sponsored by parish organizations, primarily to raise money for their treasuries. Sometimes, though, there is a special party or dance, like the one held to say goodbye to Fr. Leonard, a well-liked assistant who was reassigned, or the thank-you celebration for parishioners who had worked on last year's unusually successful festival. While such events are not included on the social calendar for the average year, they are similar to regularly scheduled affairs. Other social gatherings, like the Mother's Day dinner sponsored by the Madonna Guild, or the father and son softball game (followed by a hot dog and soft-drink lunch in the cafeteria) run by the Dad's Club, are different and will not be discussed in the paragraphs that follow. We focus instead on get-togethers for men and women.

They are always held in the gymnasium, bedecked for the occasion with brightly colored crepe paper hanging from the ceiling, with intricately designed posters on the walls, and creative center-pieces for the thirty to forty tables covered with white tablecloths. The Mardi Gras dance, held just before Lent, is noted for its exquisite decorations. Each year a theme is chosen, perhaps the roaring twenties or the bicentennial, and the gym is adorned in the appropriate decor. Several women have gained the reputation of being experts at that task and, consequently, are called upon for advice and assistance. The men also help, by climbing the high ladders, moving the basketball backboards, and setting up the tables.

These tables are arranged parallel to the stage, placed on each side of the basketball floor (which is tile, not wood) so the middle, the largest part of the playing surface, will be available for dancing. If you were to stand at the free-throw line of the basket nearest the cafeteria, looking directly in front, at the stage, you would see about twenty tables on the far left and the same number on the far right of the basketball court. And when the lights dim and the floor has been sprinkled with a substance that prevents slipping and sliding, and people begin to arrive, you know things are underway.

Also, as in the seating arrangements at a Madonna Guild meeting, there is a definite pattern as to where and with whom a couple would be placed. Indeed, the women usually plan that ahead of time and the tables are reserved for small groups. If you were to walk down the middle of the floor you would notice unobtrusive signs that say: "The Basinski's," or "The Ostrowski's." Mrs. Basinski and Mrs. Ostrowski, you may rest assured, have checked with their friends long before the event, insuring that they could spend the evening with one another. As an aside, women who engage in organizing these tight groups for a social gathering are those who are usually looked up to as leaders, of the cliques and of the parish. Each table is large enough for twenty people, of whom some are relatives while others are friends. Often a grandmother or grandfather will be invited too, which, to them, is a great honor. In total, about three hundred people usually attend.

The cook is usually engaged two months ahead of time. Several parishioners cater weddings, showers, and other affairs, both locally and throughout Detroit's Polonia. Of those, Martha Jasinski has the best reputation. In her early fifties, she is known for the fine foods she prepares, and for her competent staff of assistants who work with her as a team. Parishioners who are wondering whether to attend a dance or a party will invariably ask if Martha is doing the cooking, the response having a strong influence on their decision. However, her services are in great demand, so it is not always possible to hire her, even far in advance.

Now, once a cook has been commissioned, the menu is planned and purchasing begins. Having a special arrangement with the women who do the catering, Johnny's Market provides discounts as well as special services. Fresh kiełbasa is made, center cut pork chops are trimmed just right, and the kapusta (sauerkraut) is prepared for cooking. A special mixture of meats is ground for meatballs, its ingredients privy only to Johnny and the cook. You may ask Martha, for example, but she usually smiles and says, "I'm glad you enjoyed them."

The women who work for Martha or her competitors begin cooking one or two days before the scheduled event, especially if a large crowd is expected. Then, on the afternoon of the appointed evening, cars pull up to the rear of the gym, and the husbands help their wives carry large electric roasters of sausage, which has been boiled ready for baking. Potatoes are brought in too; they will be peeled, cooked, then mashed just before serving. Having been ready for a day, the meatballs will simmer in a special sauce of spices and mushrooms. Pie shells are delicately treated, and filled with banana cream or strawberry fillings. They are lined up on tables in the cafeteria, to be seen but not tasted until the proper time.

In fact, those attending the party who try to enter the cafeteria before serving time will be firmly told their presence is not wanted, nor appreciated. Or, they will be stared at coldly: Clearly, one does not disturb Martha or any other cook during last-minute preparations.

So people usually take their seats, have a drink or two (most functions provide the mix and ice, while the patrons bring their own liquor), talk with their friends, and wait patiently for the music to begin. Comments on the decorations, the outfits people are wearing, and who is sitting with whom are passed then. A half-hour or so after the scheduled starting time (usually around 8:00 P.M.), the four or five members of the band climb up on the stage and ready their instruments. And soon the music starts.

More often than not the band consists of an accordion, saxophone, trumpet, electric guitar, clarinet, and drums. Usually there is one musician who plays two or more instruments, and another who sings. Some bands are either all-male or all-female, while others are mixed. The musicians must be good in order to be hired. For an excellent band is even more important than the food when judging whether the evening is successful or not. Choosing, however, is made easier by the reputation groups acquire as they play for weddings and parish dances throughout Detroit's Polish-American communities. In fact, there is an unofficial but accurate ranking of the top ten bands. And at St. Thaddeus they always go for number one. They may even change the date of a social event just to accommodate a favorite group's schedule.

Now, the question arises: What makes a band popular? It boils down to its ability to play both fast and slow music with a steady, danceable beat; a wide repertoire of old and new songs; a pleasant vocalist; and an ability to obtain rapport with the audience. Albeit those are important factors, nothing can compare with one overriding concern: Can they play the polka? People don't say, "Can they play it *well?*" Their question is, "Can they *play* the polka?" For if a band doesn't do it well, with the right beat, with the clarinet coming in at the right time, then they can't play it at all.[11]

Until the first polka is played only a few couples are on the dance floor. Then, suddenly, there is a change. People rush for preferred partners. Grandmas and Grandpas ease themselves off their seats and straighten their backs as they move toward the floor. Some of the women dance with one another; fathers take a turn with their daughters, and sons with their mothers. Soon, there is barely enough room to spin quickly around while circling the entire floor, to stamp your feet to the music, to twirl your partner, *to do the polka.* But within moments, it seems, it is all over. Handkerchiefs work profusely to wipe away the perspiration. "Never again," people say, "that's just too much!" Then, knowing how they feel, the band plays a slow tune. When the dancers have had time to recuperate, the polka begins again.

And within an hour the setting has transformed. The small cliques have disappeared. Everyone is mingling, having a good time, forgetting about the vicissitudes of their daily lives, leaving behind their problems. The pastor moves through the crowd, stopping at every table, catching up on the latest gossip.

Now a hush pervades the room. Guests can hear the incipient strains of a familiar tune—Bobby Vinton's "Melody of Love," a song he wrote and recorded to celebrate his heritage. Because half the lyrics are in Polish, Bobby Vinton became a hero to Polish Americans. On this night it makes the parishioners of St. Thaddeus happy and proud. Women are crying. Yet everyone is singing. The band soon finishes, but then answers the many pleas to play it again. There are some tears, more singing, more joy, and a sense of camaraderie.

About ten o'clock the meal is served. There is more than enough food for everyone, and it is all prepared to perfection. It is difficult not to overeat. "But then," people say, "with all that dancing, what harm can it do? You've burned up plenty of calories already, and the night is still young. So enjoy!" And they do.

Dancing continues until an hour or two past midnight. (Once, when a member of the Dad's Club passed the hat to pay the band for another hour of music, he collected more than a hundred dollars, for which the musicians stayed until two in the morning. However, that is unusual.) Then, as the band completes packing up its gear, the committee who sponsored the event starts cleaning up. Others pitch in, and in an hour, the gymnasium becomes spick-and-span again. The tables and chairs are folded up, the floor is swept, and decorations are taken down. By this time the cook and her assistants have finished their work too; they allow people into the cafeteria to accept their praises, here and there dishing out an extra piece of pie.

At this juncture folks head for home. Most of them have attended the Saturday evening mass, before the dance, so they are looking forward to a lazy and enjoyable Sunday morning. Then the reminiscing begins, and it goes on until the next social event at St. Thaddeus.

THE PARISH SCHOOL

From its beginning St. Thaddeus has provided an elementary school education for its children. Indeed, one of the primary reasons Polish Americans founded the parish was to insure for them a Catholic education that stressed Polish cultural traditions and heritage. Classes began soon after the construction of the first church, a wooden structure that also served as a school from Monday through Friday. The first teachers were the pastor, Fr. Kaminski, and two female parishioners. Reading, English, and arithmetic were taught, along with the history and geography of the United States. Students also studied the Polish language and learned about Poland. Older parishioners have fond memories of attending school in those wooden-church days. The classes were large, they say, and discipline was strict, but one was certain to learn the three Rs. And while lessons were taught in English, the same former students remember being more comfortable speaking Polish, the language spoken at home.

In 1926 construction was completed on a brick structure designed to function as a church, school, and convent. With the arrival of thirteen teaching nuns the parish elementary school was in full operation. In its first full year, 1926, the school had 706 in grades one to eight. Throughout the thirties and forties enrollment remained between five and seven hundred. But in 1953 it climbed to an all-time high of 837. During the latter part of the fifties school enrollment declined slightly, yet it continued to hover around seven hundred. However, since 1961 the median age of the community has been increasing, resulting in a steadily decreasing number of school-age children. Thus, school registration also declined, from 658 in that year to a record low of 292 in 1972.

Despite the smaller enrollment, and an increase in operating costs—due partly to the salaries of lay teachers, who have been hired because of a shortage of teaching nuns—the school remains an integral part of St. Thaddeus. In fact, parishioners sponsor an annual festival to raise money for it. And while some complain about being asked to sell raffle tickets and donate their time to work at the three-day event, a large number participate because they feel the school should remain open at all costs. And there are two separate but related reasons why.

First, mothers and fathers place great value on educating their children in an environment that not only includes religious instruction but also the firm discipline so characteristic of Catholic schools. They want their youngsters to acquire the knowledge and skills to be successful, which to them also means being a good Catholic and following the rules of the church. Sending a child to a public school is viewed as a risk: he or she might lose interest in religion by not being exposed to the church's teachings on a regular basis during the formative years. As practicing Catholics most parents feel strongly that it is their duty to provide an appropriate education. Some, though a minority, go even further. They believe it is a sin to enroll their children in a public school, and remind you of how they came to believe that. "It was the priests who taught us it was a sin," said a mother of two pre-teenagers. "Years ago they said it was a mortal sin if we had the money and didn't send the kids to Catholic school. And I don't know, I guess I still think that way."

"You're damn right," added her husband. "Why I remember a bishop here in Detroit who said we could be excommunicated for not following that rule, and that sticks in my mind." While that couple is not alone, the more general attitude in St. Thaddeus is that sending children to Catholic school is done more out of duty than from fear of sin.

Most adults, even those without school-age children, have an

additional motive in attempting to save the school. The president
of a parish organization explains:

> If our school closes people will run from the neighborhood and buy
> homes in the suburbs. Let's not kid ourselves; what keeps people
> here ain't just the church, it's the school! That's why we gotta keep
> having those festivals—to keep the neighborhood alive. If we close
> the school, one thing's for sure: the neighborhood will die.

So the school is seen as the key to not only maintaining a Polish-
American community, but one located in a predominantly Black
city. For the assumption people make is that a neighborhood without a Catholic school tends to drive current residents to the suburbs
to seek what they consider a proper education. People also assume
that without the school it would be difficult to attract new Polish-
American residents, and they believe that in time that would mean
a different kind of neighborhood, a Black neighborhood.

While this is a complex issue that will be discussed in the
following chapter, it is important to mention here that those who
live in the neighborhood want to stay. Yet it is doubtful they will if
the community becomes predominantly Black, rather than Polish,
for that is precisely what has happened in other Polish-American
parishes in Detroit, especially those whose schools have been
closed. The members of St. Thaddeus are aware of that, and this
is why, in a very real sense, to them the school *is* the community.

But what of the school itself? What and how do children learn?
And what are the teachers like; how do they interact with students
and one another? For answers to those questions let us look in on a
classroom, mindful that the description is based on my having
taught and observed the seventh and eighth grades at St. Thaddeus.

The physical setting of the classroom is traditional. The
teacher's desk occupies a prominent position up front, facing four
or five parallel rows of students seated on brightly varnished
wooden chairs, each with a small desk top attached for writing and
other school work. A large crucifix is hanging near the top of the
front wall, and right below it is a clock. Still lower, at about
eye-level, is an old chalkboard that has recently been painted to
hide its age and provide a better writing surface. There are radia-
tors along the rear wall, located beneath large windows, some of

which have been broken and replaced with acrylic panes. Narrow bulletin boards of a cork-like surface line the two remaining walls, and are covered with posters made by students in their art class. Also, pictures of saints are placed there by the teacher.

At this school the students change classes, so the teacher remains in a homeroom, which normally includes from thirty to thirty-five students.

They begin to arrive at about 8:15 in the morning. The boys are dressed in dark blue pants and light blue shirts with dark, solid-colored ties. Their hair is fairly short and, because of the dress code, must not touch their collars or cover their ears. Nor are boots of any kind allowed. The girls wear green plaid jumpers with white blouses. Most have on dark green knee socks and dark shoes, though oxfords and saddles are worn by some. Their skirts are no more than two inches above the knees, according to dress code regulations, but a few girls get away with four, especially those who are less physically developed.

When students enter the classroom they go to their assigned seats, boys on one side, girls on the other. While several boys watch for the arrival of the teacher, others talk and joke with one another sometimes quite loudly. Then, when the "lookout" spots the teacher coming down the hall, the students lower their voices and settle down. By the time the teacher enters the classroom, there is silence.

At 8:25 the bell rings and the students rise in unison, face the crucifix, and begin the Our Father. The Pledge of Allegiance is next, followed by several announcements from the teacher. At 8:30 classes change.

During the course of a typical day, seventh and eighth graders will study the following subjects: English, reading, mathematics, history, science, and religion. Classes on art, music, and physical education are held once a week, usually on Fridays.

When I taught in the school I was one of four seventh- and eighth-grade teachers, three of whom were lay persons. Two of the three lay teachers were third-generation Polish Americans, as was the young nun responsible for all religion classes. The remaining subjects were divided up evenly among all of us.

Discipline was strict, and most teachers felt it was necessary to make students afraid of them in order to establish and maintain control. My notes on a conversation among teachers shows how they feel about the matter:

All the lay teachers were gathered in the faculty room to have lunch. The room is nicely furnished (thanks to the Madonna Guild) with comfortable upholstered chairs and a coffeepot. The nuns are having lunch in the convent, as usual.

Today, students are the topic of conversation. One of the teachers, a third-generation Polish American from a working-class family, says "by and large the kids are not too smart. I mean they seem curious when they are young, but I'll be damned if I know what happens to them when they grow up. Somehow they lose their curiosity. Then they become disinterested, lazy, and not very bright. My guess is it's their parents—they just don't care about the kids."

"It's not that," said another, also a third-generation Pole, "it's fear. Somehow these students aren't afraid anymore, that's the real problem. Fear has to be instilled at an early age."

The first teacher concurs. "Yup," he says, "you hit the nail on the head. Fear is everywhere in the world. Why, it's man's driving force. Why do you think people stop for a red light? They're afraid of getting a ticket, that's why. So you are absolutely right. What we have to do is make the kids afraid of us; then they will do what we want."

The third teacher also agreed, but she had some additional points to make. "You can get a degree in education today, but nobody tells you how to deal with the dummies, the ones who misbehave. Permissiveness, that's the big thing nowadays. Let the students do what they want, as long as they are learning. That wouldn't work in this school. You gotta show the kids who's boss. You gotta force them to learn and behave. Forget what the experts say. This isn't a summer camp we're running here; by God, it's a school!"

While students complain about harsh teachers and rigid discipline, they do know what to expect from those in charge. And they feel more comfortable if new teachers conform to the behavior expected of someone in that role. Given my own very different philosophy of education and mode of teaching, it is understandable that the students had problems with me and I with them. One of my seventh graders provided some insight, in a polite manner, into what was a frustrating situation for all concerned:

Mr. Wrobel, may I say something to you? You've been here two months now, and the kids don't know what to think. I mean they think you're okay, but they don't know if you like them, if you care about them. I mean you don't get angry and scream at us. We were talking about this the other day, and you know what Teddy said? He said "Gee, I wish that Mr. Wrobel would haul off and slug somebody one of these days, then everything would be okay." And you know something, Mr. Wrobel? Teddy's right. If you followed his advice we would all know where you stand.

My mistake, then, was in attempting to introduce change into a long-established cultural system. Furthermore, the teaching methods and strategies I brought to St. Thaddeus reflected my own values, not those of the community. Later, through conversations with parents, I learned why they preferred a school that emphasized order and discipline.

A father of three young boys, one of whom was my student, told me how he and others felt about the matter:

You're damn right we like it the way it is. Why do you think we send our kids to St. Thaddeus? Do you know what's happening in other schools, the public ones? Why kids slug their teachers and smoke grass in the bathrooms. Those schools are "blackboard jungles," and there ain't no learning going on. Our kids learn stuff, and they also learn how to behave and respect their elders.

Another factor is the strong desire to raise children who will be successful in the outside world and, related, are parental assumptions about the child-rearing patterns and teaching styles best suited to that goal, as discussed in the previous chapter. "We can only do so much at home," said one mother, "and since we didn't even finish high school, my husband and I depend on the teachers to teach the kids what they need to know. We'll make sure the kids listen and behave, but it's the teacher who's gotta teach." Once again, Lillian Rubin has analyzed such an attitude with great insight: "Feeling inadequate and lacking confidence that they can pass on their slim skills to their children, [working-class parents] demand that the schools enforce discipline in the belief that only then will their children learn all that they themselves did not."[12]

Yet there is another side to the story. Parents from all social classes and all parts of the country are raising serious questions about what *Newsweek* called "the flaccid standards of public schools," and searching for institutions with "strict codes of conduct."[13] Indeed, a recent front-page story in *The Detroit Free Press*, with the headline "Back to Basics in School is a Big Hit," reports on seventeen schools in Philadelphia "emphasizing discipline, the 3R's and patriotism."[14] While the school board in that city had originally planned to begin the new program in one school, "officials said they received almost 5,000 applications from parents wanting their children to attend the school and decided to add 16 schools to the program."[15] In trying to understand St. Thaddeus school, then, we should keep in mind the growing dissatisfaction with what are often considered more modern institutions.

And perhaps we should listen to those who were raised in traditional Catholic schools and later wrote about that experience, like the columnist Jim Bishop:

> The Black Swans of the classroom. They had neither feet nor legs. They floated silently, peering at students from behind white corrugations. The voices were clinical in detachment. Teaching nuns. . . .
>
> I attended a Catholic primary school. It was a lesson in surviving fright. The teacher never had time to exude love or compassion. The one she reserved for God, the second for the poor and the weak. . . .
>
> She was a cattle drover; a teacher; a judge; a passport to knowledge; the silent, lonely heart; the executioner. She seldom used a ruler to measure anything except the distance between a long overhand swing and a student's hand. . . .
>
> All the teachers cared about were the fundamentals. We were taught our prayers, our religion, about sin, tolerance for others, and punishment. We were doomed if we did this, touched that, stole a trinket, or disobeyed our parents. It was a no-win situation, lasting eight years. . . .
>
> I grew up to love one—Sister Marie Alacoque, who taught me in the third grade. A note arrived from her the other day. She and seven others were astounded that I had a career, a calling. "Jim," she writes, "do keep up the good work. I love your writings on Big John. He was wonderful."
>
> Forget the religious aspects. By God, they were teachers.[16]

While that is true, some graduates of St. Thaddeus who have moved on to college are ambivalent about their experience, not because of what they learned, but how it was taught. One young man now attending Wayne State University said:

When I was in grade school everybody told me what to do. I was afraid to say anything in class because I thought I might be wrong. Oh, I got good grades, all right, but I wasn't learning how to think for myself. Then I went on to a small Catholic high school with exactly the same kind of environment. Now, in college, I'm on my own, and it's a pretty frightening experience. Maybe I should have gone to a small Catholic college. But there was no way the family could have managed that.

In summary, most parents are pleased with the education their children receive at St. Thaddeus. And they are proud of the fact that students from the school recently ranked first, second, and third in the sophomore class of a well-known and academically superior Catholic high school that attracts primarily Polish Americans. Yet how children learn does create problems for some who leave the parish and neighborhood to go on to college. For growing up and receiving an education in a Polish-American community and later encountering the larger society is indeed a cross-cultural experience.

POLISH–AMERICAN CULTURE

National parishes were established for ethnic groups so their members might worship in a cultural milieu that reflects the heritage and traditions of the old country. But today, the members of St. Thaddeus do not identify with Poland, nor do they refer to themselves as "Polish." "My grandparents left Poland because they wanted a better way of life," said one parishioner. "And that means Poland wasn't a very good place to live at the time. So what do I care what happens over there? It ain't my country. I'm not Polish, I'm a Polish American." Earlier in this work we suggested that Polish-American culture represented something more than a combination of Polish and American elements. Now it is time to address that matter at greater length, paying special attention to the role of the parish.

While it is possible to get along adequately in the subject community without speaking a word of English, the majority of the third- and fourth-generation do not speak Polish. Nor is the language taught in the parish school, as it once was. For according to the nuns and parishioners who recall the incident, the parents of schoolchildren protested the teaching of Polish in the 1950s, and asked that their boys and girls spend more time on "relevant subjects": math, spelling, and English composition. Although some mothers and fathers were dissatisfied with the decision to drop Polish from the curriculum, and proceeded to enroll their children in special language classes run by the Polish Women's Alliance, it appears that the majority favored the move. And since then, there has only been one year that Polish was taught in the school as a regular subject, reportedly by an assistant priest who had just arrived from Poland. Today students receive no language training and no information on the old country. Indeed, some of the lay teachers consider it a waste of time to study Polish history and culture.

But the church differs from the school with regard to language. Each Sunday two masses are said in Polish, complete with the reading of the gospel, a sermon, and the usual announcements. Those masses are well-attended by members of the first and second generation. And for these parishioners, confessions in Polish are heard regularly by the pastor and his assistants. The sons and daughters of immigrants report they find it easier to confess in Polish, even though English is their first language. "When you tell the priest a sin in Polish," one man told me, "somehow it doesn't seem as bad."

In addition to language, the church is also instrumental in preserving certain Polish customs that revolve around religious worship. For example, Christ's tomb is displayed on Good Friday, and Easter baskets filled with food are blessed on Holy Saturday. Polish carols—"Kolędy"—are sung on Christmas Eve and throughout the holiday season, and wafers—"Opłatki"—are distributed so parishioners may share them with their friends and relatives at "Wigilja," a traditional Christmas Eve supper. On the other hand, Fr. Kaminski has complained publicly about poor attendance at Corpus Christi celebrations, an important feast day to Poles. Still, Polish religious customs are popular among parishioners, even those of the third and fourth generation.

Also common is a tradition known as "Stypa," a feast that includes food and drinks immediately following a funeral. "Poprawiny," a "second celebration" the day after a wedding (usually held at the home of the bride), has become less important during the past twenty years, but often followed is the time-honored practice of greeting the bride and groom with salt and bread when they return from the church to begin the wedding celebration.

In summary, Polish traditions are retained in some dimensions of parish life. But one should not conclude that the members of St. Thaddeus are assimilated because changes have taken place, or because customs followed in the old country are no longer as important as they once were. For such an opinion neglects the fact that Polish Americans are a distinct ethnic group with their own way of life, a system of values and behavioral patterns only partially based on their Polish heritage.

The polkas played at parish social functions are not strictly Polish, nor are they American. Indeed, the folklore that surrounds the polka in this country, including myths and legends about certain bands, the cultural significance of lyrics, the radio stations which feature this music, and even the intense competition among groups, is something very Polish-American. And so is the food served at an event like that we described earlier, as is the role of cooks in a Polish-American community.

But perhaps more important, the culture of Polish-Americans is reflected in the emphasis on the family, the parish, and the neighborhood as social units. The importance of orderliness, the value placed on home and property, the way husbands and wives relate to one another and their children, the theme of sacrifice, these are all elements of Polish-American working-class culture. And that culture will be transmitted to succeeding generations usually in ways that are difficult to measure from a strictly scientific point of view.

What does the above have to do with the parish? Simply this: By establishing and maintaining a community, St. Thaddeus provides for the development, preservation, and continual growth of Polish-American culture.

The Neighborhood 6

In an earlier chapter the neighborhood was described as a network of nuclear families linked together through mutual participation in the parish and residence in a specific geographic area. We used the phrase "latent neighborliness" to characterize social interaction, suggesting that neighbors are friends without being friendly, that everybody knows someone who knows someone else. But the neighborhood was also depicted as a pleasant place to live, a section of the city with tree-lined streets, freshly painted homes, and carefully groomed lawns; a place with shops and stores catering to the needs, wants, and desires of a Polish-American clientele.

Yet that idyllic picture is somewhat misleading. For in recent years life in the subject neighborhood has left much to be desired. Indeed, many are dissatisfied with the situation and perplexed about whether or not to stay there. In fact, what has happened in the past several years is a very real threat to the survival of a vibrant ethnic community. What has happened, and why? Is there anything that can be done? These are questions of paramount importance to those who live here, but they should also be of great interest to social scientists as well as policy makers concerned with the future of our cities.

We begin with an essay written by Casimer Matulewicz, a student of mine in the seventh grade of the parish school. I asked Casimer, aged twelve, to describe his neighborhood, to tell me what it meant to him. But what he wrote does much more than that. It captures both the meaning and mood of the community.

What does my neighborhood mean to me? It means that when I walk to school in the morning I see Mrs. Baranski sweeping the porch or

121

weeding the lawn. She is my next-door neighbor. She works very hard to keep her house clean. So do the other neighbors.

Do you know that I know the names of the people who live in all the houses I pass on the way to school? I know these people because I see them at church. I know Mr. Ted because he's our scout leader. I know Mr. Frank because he's an usher in the church. Sometimes when I come from school I see Mrs. Zieleniewski. She's real nice. She works at the parish festival to get money for the school.

The kids in the neighborhood are pretty nice. Mostly we play outside because mothers yell at us for messing up the houses. My best friend is Jerry. He lives close to Johnny's Market. That's five blocks from my house. He comes over to my house every day, or I go to his house to call him out. Sometimes we go to the drive-in for a coke.

My Ma and Dad like our neighborhood but they might move. I don't want to move because of Jerry and the other guys from school, but if Ma and Dad say move we will move. They are scared of this neighborhood. They say there are too many people getting ripped off around here. Did you hear about Tommy's Dad? He was beaten up over by the "projects." Did you hear about my Ma having her purse stolen? It happened when she was coming from a meeting at church. Dad was really mad. That's when he started talking about moving. He and Ma are still talking about it.

CRIME

Casimer's parents are not alone. Every couple I interviewed, and most with whom I came in contact, have considered moving. And while the majority have opted to stay, their decision is by no means a final one. Art Krogulecki, a foreman at the Dodge assembly plant and father of four, tells us why:

I ain't moving. I was born in this house forty-one years ago and right here is where I'm gonna stay. In the last three years I put four thousand dollars into fixing up the place. Did all the work myself. And now, after all these years, the place is just what we wanted. We're close to the church, school, bus lines, and it ain't too far from work. So why should we move? The suburbs don't offer us nothing we can't get here. But I'll tell you something: If crime gets any worse around here I ain't gonna have no choice. It's my job to protect the family, and when I can't do that we'll get the hell outta here.

Like a host of others, Art Krogulecki has adopted a wait-and-see attitude. But nothing would change that approach more abruptly than a heightening of the crime rate. Already the figures would stagger one: from 1966 to 1973 crime in the neighborhood has increased more than 100 percent.[1] And that does not include the numerous unreported purse snatchings and bike thefts. Nor do statistics of any kind convey how crime evokes hostility, fear, and suspicion on the part of residents, both victims and those who wonder if, or when, they will be next. And how well I know those feelings; our rented house was burglarized three times during the summer of 1972. My field notes, written the day after the last robbery, show my reaction:

It happened again, the third time within three months. But this one was different: the burglars got in through the back door. They used a crowbar, I think, because the door molding was ripped right off the wall, and the two chain locks were busted. Last time it was through the basement window. I guess my nailing those windows shut was effective. But really, if someone wants to break in, they will. Nails and locks only serve to slow them down a little.

They left the radio, electric typewriter, TV and camera, but took thirty dollars I had in a dresser and my African coin collection. The bedroom was a mess. Dresser drawers strewn all over the place, pictures off the walls, mattress on the floor. Even the rug was rolled up. They were very thorough.

I don't know when I've been so angry. God, would I like to get my hands on whoever did this. The dirty bastards. Who in the hell do they think they are coming into our home. Especially the bedroom. That's a private place. But then everything we have here is an extension of ourselves, so it's like being violated.

Now I know how the people in this neighborhood feel. When I first came here I laughed at the bars on the windows and the reluctance to take vacations. No more. I feel like nailing two-by-fours across the back door and just sealing it shut.

I used to think it was silly to be suspicious of strangers who walked down the street. No more. Now I too suspect people I don't know. Hell, they could be casing the place.

But I really worry about someone breaking in when I'm away and Kathy and the kids are home alone. What would happen if the burglars tried something at night, when everyone was asleep? I don't know. Perhaps we shouldn't think about it.

But we did. And for some time my wife and I seriously considered moving. Yet we decided to stay. We went out less often, and were more cautious; and, as a final precaution, my family stayed with friends or relatives when I was out of town.

Meanwhile, burglaries are only part of the total picture. What is more worrisome to parents is the vulnerability of their children. So when small packs of young strangers run through the neighborhood, knocking kids off their two-wheelers or ten-speeds, it is not just a missing bike that upsets parents. It is the possibility a son or daughter might be injured, perhaps seriously, while innocently riding around the block. And, clearly, that is a realistic fear. For six blocks from the church, a Polish-American teenager from a nearby parish was shot in the head and killed by a group of young Black males who surrounded him and demanded his bicycle. While an incident that vicious is uncommon, many school children from St. Thaddeus have been beaten up before their bikes were stolen. As a result, some boys and girls are no longer allowed to own two-wheelers, and others must follow strict rules regarding where or when they can use them.

Concern for the safety of their children is what prompted residents to speak out against crime in the neighborhood. And that reached its peak after two teenage girls had their winter coats stolen on successive days. Two Black men had followed them from the bus stop, jumped out of their car, and demanded the garments at gunpoint. The following morning a meeting was held in the basement of the rectory to discuss the situation. After a protest was lodged at the local police station, the inspector in charge of the precinct agreed to attend a complaint session in the parish activities building.

Nearly three hundred people came. They began arriving a half-hour before the meeting was scheduled to start: neighbors, parents and children, senior citizens, priests and nuns: all of them grim-faced and apprehensive, some angry, few hopeful. The inspector walked into the room with the pastor and climbed the stairs leading up to the stage, where two chairs and a microphone had been placed. Fr. Bulakowski spoke first. He summarized why the meeting had been called, and introduced Inspector Arendt. The police officer had a way with people. He told of how his own house was robbed, how he and his wife felt safer with a watchdog, how crooks were "fearless to rip-off a cop's place." Then he asked, "How many of you sitting here tonight have been victims of crime in the last year?"

At least 75 percent of those in attendance raised their hands. And for the next hour and a half people told the policeman their stories. An elderly widow in her mid-seventies described how she was mugged on her way home from bingo night. Several young Black males had hidden under a car parked near the gymnasium, waiting. It was over very quickly, but the woman lost her purse and received a broken hip. A father of four boys said his children had a total of nine bikes stolen in the last two years, and wanted to know why it wasn't possible for kids to ride around the block without being afraid. A white-haired gentleman with a heavy accent got up and complained that he could no longer walk to the corner for a Polish newspaper and an ice-cream cone: "I've done it every night for the last twenty years," he said. "Now they steal my change and push me around, so I'm afraid to leave the house." On went the vivid descriptions, evoking sadness and anger. Inspector Arendt was sympathetic, but he was not surprised. "It's happening all over the city," he said, "primarily because of the drug problem."

"We know that," shouted a woman from the audience, "but what we want you to tell us is how you can help us right here in this neighborhood." The officer listened politely, paused briefly, then began:

We want to help you out, but we just don't have enough patrol cars. Sure, I can increase the patrol in this area for a while—and I intend to do just that—but then another area of my precinct will begin to complain and I'll have to give them some attention. So I want you to know that one of our major problems is the way judges in this city work. We catch young thugs and the judges turn them loose because they say we don't have enough evidence. Then they're right back on the streets to commit other crimes.

But the audience wasn't satisfied. "There must be *some* way to attack the problem," said a president of a parish organization. "Well, there is," responded the inspector.

> But it's up to you. You can do a lot by leaving a light on when you go out or getting one of those automatic timing devices that turns on the lights when you're not home. We have one of those and it works pretty good. But what is really important here is to be careful about your patterns of movement. I mean, don't go out at the same time two days in a row, because these guys are sharp, and they'll be watching. So change your habits; go out in the morning one day, the afternoon the next, and so on. And try not to leave the house totally empty. If somebody from the family can't stay home, then get a dog that barks like hell. And be good neighbors. If you see something suspicious going on next door, or if a stranger is lurking around, give us a call. We'll try to be there as soon as possible.

While the representative of the police department meant well, he was not reassuring to the parishioners. "What the hell," remarked one man as we left the building, "here's a cop telling us he's got problems dealing with crime, and that's his job. We pay taxes to be protected and the guy tells us to buy new locks and get a dog. It's the same old shit. What a helluva way to run a city." Still, many followed the officer's recommendations. But none of those measures have displaced the fear, the everpresent feeling that tomorrow, or perhaps the next day, you or one of your family members might be victimized. And for some, like Cass Lisiecki, that is no way to live. Cass told me about his decision to move to Warren, a nearby suburb.

> We've had it. Even though we haven't been robbed yet, it could happen any day now. The neighbors on both sides have gotten it, and so have families down the street. But it ain't just the burglaries that scare me, it's knowing that it ain't safe around here anymore. The whole neighborhood has changed. Christine, our seventh grader, was beaten up three times on her way to school. It was those colored kids from the projects that did it. Now we have to walk her half way to school, and that's a helluva thing to have to do. We live right across the street from the projects, and we're all scared. You know what the mothers on this street do when the kids want to visit each other? They stand on their porches and tell the

kids to run as fast as they can from one house to another. This is so the mothers can make sure the kids don't get jumped. When I saw the wife doing that, I said "let's get the hell outta here," and that's just what we are doing.

Yet when fear of crime drives a Polish-American family from the ethnic neighborhood, some observers are quick to label them racists. Andrew Greeley has put the matter in proper perspective:

> There is a strong tendency in contemporary social policy to assume that once the magic word "racism" is uttered all need for further understanding—to say nothing of compassion—has been eliminated. There may be every reason to suspect that bigotry lurks in every human personality (although the objects of bigotry may vary); it may be that some of the fears of certain segments of the population have a basis in reality; it may be indeed, that the very term "racism" has become broad enough to include so many meanings that it now means nothing. However, it is only pragmatic wisdom that if one is going to have to deal with certain ethnic groups, one must attempt to understand the causes of the responses of those groups to racial issues. To write them off as racist and be done with them may well be socially and politically counterproductive. [2]

The immediate issue here is not a racial one. But it is race-related: the firm conclusion drawn by parishioners is that young Black males are primarily responsible for the dramatic increase in the neighborhood crime rate. They make that judgment by what they see and hear.

Many have observed Black youths stealing purses and bicycles and beating-up children from St. Thaddeus school. And some have surprised Blacks attempting to burglarize homes or cars. Then, there are the victims of muggings and other street crimes who have stood face-to-face with their assailants. What these parishioners have seen and experienced is sure to be heard by most members of St. Thaddeus. The efficient network described earlier gathers such information and quickly transmits it, much like a special announcement that interrupts regular programming on radio and TV. And what listeners hear is the details of the particular crime, as well as the ethnic identity of the criminal. Most of the time, he is a young Black male.

Some of those juvenile offenders are believed to be from the

predominantly Black public housing project, located directly
across from the southern boundary of the neighborhood, and referred to as "the projects." Bicycles stolen from school children are
often spotted there, being ridden by those identified as the alleged
thieves. Furthermore, that locale is the scene of many crimes.
You will remember that Casimer Matulewicz mentioned it in his
essay, as did Cass Lisiecki, when he told us why he was moving to
Warren. Now, parishioners avoid the area and are cautious when-
ever they cannot.

The above notwithstanding, they do not blame all crime on the
young residents of the housing project. Nor do they generalize,
contrary to public opinion, about the Black population of the city.
"It's the young hoodlums," said a mother whose son was robbed
by three Black teenagers.

> They are the ones who are ruining this neighborhood. It ain't the
> Black people who live here among us that are committing the
> crimes, not the homeowners. It's the young toughs from the proj-
> ects or those punks from the west side who want money so they can
> buy drugs. Those are the real troublemakers.

A similar distinction was made when a group of mothers met in
the rectory prior to the demonstration at the police station:

> It ain't my Black neighbors, they're okay. And so are all the other
> Black homeowners in the neighborhood. We get along just fine. It's
> the "young punks" and men who don't work that are bothering us.
> Black people who have jobs are not the problem.

> Yeah, you're right. That's why if we want to do something about
> crime in the neighborhood, we gotta involve the colored home-
> owners. They're just as scared as us.

> I agree. What we're talking about here is keeping the neighborhood
> a nice place to live. And that means getting all the concerned
> people together, white and colored.

So, other categories besides race are used when discussing who
is responsible for crime in the neighborhood. Blacks who live there
are described as "homeowners," "working people," or "people just
like us." It is young Black males, and more specifically, "juvenile
delinquents," "punks who don't work," "kids who quit school," or

"young toughs into the drug scene" at whom parishioners direct
their hostility. And while Polish Americans may understand the
social and economic reasons behind juvenile delinquency and
crime, that does not justify it, they say. John Skorupski expresses
the prevailing point of view:

> You read the papers and watch TV programs about Black people
> having a tough time getting jobs, good houses, and a decent educa-
> tion. The kids ain't got no future so they turn to crime. Hell, I can
> understand how that works. But dammit, understanding is one
> thing. What am I to do when my house gets robbed or the wife gets
> mugged? Feel sorry for the guy who committed the crime? Just
> because he's Black? No way! No sir, crime is crime, no matter
> what. That's how I feel, and nobody is going to change my attitude.

In short, sociological explanations that crime is an effect rather
than a cause, that it results from unemployment, inadequate education, and a host of other factors, means little or nothing to the
victims (or potential victims) of muggings and burglaries.[3] It is one
thing to be aware of social inequities, and, as Andrew Hacker has
suggested, "quite another to regard the man nudging a knife into
your ribs as someone to whom society offered no other choice."[4]

Still, a working-class Polish American's desire for "law and
order," his pleas for a safe and secure neighborhood, are often
interpreted as a subtle form of irrational racism. That reaction, I
suggest, may just be another way of "blaming the victim," a scape-
goat mechanism, if you will. For when observers argue that the
problem lies in the hearts and minds of Polish Americans, and say
it is basically psychological in origin, then key political and business leaders can low-key the social, political, and economic factors
that lie behind inter-ethnic animosities on the urban scene. Furthermore, as Richard Krickus points out, "the propensity to inter-
pret our urban malaise from a racial perspective accounts for the
failure to focus on the problems common to white and Black
urbanites alike."[5]

We must keep in mind, then, the results of a 1975 *Detroit Free
Press* poll:

> Half of Detroit's families would move out of the city if they could
> afford to . . . 55 percent of whites and 43 percent of blacks said

they would leave. More Blacks (36 percent) than whites (26 percent) said crime was the reason for wanting to leave Detroit.[6]

Thus, what we have been describing is not merely a problem to Polish Americans in one particular neighborhood, but a concern of many Detroit residents. The parishioners of St. Thaddeus know this. And that is why they resent being labeled "blue-collar bigots" when they complain about crime and violence.

So far we have focused on the relationship between crime and people's feelings about the neighborhood, especially with regard to staying or moving. But there are other factors that enter into such a decision. And one that has received very little attention is the role of real estate dealers, who are often referred to by neighborhood residents as "panic-peddlers."

REAL ESTATE PRACTICES

My own experiences with real estate firms is a case in point. When I was looking for a house to rent in the neighborhood I visited a local agency to see if they could be of any assistance. One of their well-dressed salesmen listened to my request, and responded:

> So you want to rent in the St. Thaddeus neighborhood, eh? Are you sure about that? Don't you know it's a "changing" neighborhood? Why before you know it, the neighborhood won't be as nice as it is now. Anyhow, we can't help you out. We want people to buy, not rent. That's how we make our money.

Based on that encounter I went to another agency, but now I pretended to be interested in purchasing a home. I wanted to see if my request elicited a similar response. It did. "What are you, an investor or something?" queried a salesman. I shook my head and explained that I was interested in the St. Thaddeus neighborhood simply because it seemed like an ideal place to live. The man looked puzzled, leaned back in his chair, and became very serious:

> But a young guy like you belongs in Warren, not in Detroit. I guess we might be able to help you out if you're really serious. But do you know that's a "mixed neighborhood"? Are you sure you and your family want to live there?

From those and similar experiences I concluded that real estate firms engage in what is known as "steering," in this case a systematic attempt to direct young white families into the suburbs.[7] Although I have no direct evidence, it seems likely that Black families are encouraged to stay away from the suburbs, and to purchase homes in certain sections of the city. Obviously, that has a great deal to do with the residential patterns of ethnic groups in the Detroit metropolitan area.

But in addition to "steering," real estate companies also take part in "blockbusting."[8] Originally the latter term meant moving a Black family on to an all-white block. Now it is commonly used to describe the practice of soliciting clients, or encouraging the white residents of an area to sell their homes. While the agents who engage in "blockbusting" often mention to prospective sellers that their neighborhood is "changing," or that "they" (meaning Blacks) are coming, such is not always the case. Nevertheless, homeowners from some of Detroit's west side communities have filed a federal suit against fifteen real estate firms, charging that "while no direct reference was made to race, the solicitation was made in an atmosphere charged with racial tensions and is causing panic, rumors, and racially motivated listings."[9] But regardless of the particular methods used in soliciting business, the fact remains that real estate agents are attempting to induce white homeowners to leave an area, en masse, in the hopes of making a profit on the resale of their homes. The following paragraphs describe how real estate salesmen go about that sort of practice.

Every homeowner, as well as those renting houses, continuously receives literature from real estate firms, through the mail and by delivery on their doorsteps. One of the more popular forms of advertising, and surely the most devastating, is a one-page flyer from one of the large companies with the words SOLD—SOLD—SOLD across the top in bold letters. Under that heading is a list of nearly two hundred homes (by street and address) sold by this firm in the general area. The list is not dated, nor is there any indication of the time period during which these homes were sold. But the implicit message it carries is clear: "Look how many people are moving from the northeast side of town; that many people can't be wrong, so you had better sell too." The listing of streets and addresses takes up almost the entire 8½ × 11 page, with a picture of the company's main office in the upper right hand corner, and the following three sentences along the bottom:

I can sell *your* house too.

I can add *your* home to this list.

I can give *you* top $.

Finally, a telephone number and the name of an agent are included.

In addition to that piece of advertising, residents receive numerous other handbills, some of which pose the following questions:

Do I know who I will let in my house?

Do I know real estate is a complicated profession?

Do I know what the buying public wants?

Do I know the best mortgage sources?

And so on. Thus, while one flyer attempts to scare the residents into selling because "everybody is doing it," another stresses that they lack the knowledge and experience to assume their own responsibility for selling their homes. That is why this sort of approach by real estate firms is a double-edged sword: you'll be in trouble if you don't sell, and you'll be in trouble if you do, especially without our help. The latter point is important because if a homeowner decides to handle the sale himself, the whole purpose of solicitation by scare tactics would backfire, for the agent would lose an opportunity to make a profit.

But handbills are one thing. More important are solicitations by phone and in person. I have had numerous telephone calls from real estate salesmen over a two-year period. At first I listened to what they had to say for purposes of the study, then later in my stay I threatened to sue if the calls didn't stop. A typical call from a real estate agent went like this:

Hello, Mr. Wrobel, this is Smith and Chester Realty. We've been admiring your house for some time now, and we've noticed that people in your area seem unusually ready to sell at this time. We think they are smart for selling. How about you? You know, we are very experienced in your area—we know what people want. So I can guarantee you a good price. Shall I set up an appointment?

While salesmen don't argue if a homeowner says he has no intention of selling, they will phone on a regular basis in an attempt to change his mind.

Less common but more effective than phone calls are face-to-face encounters between agents and residents. Real estate salesmen have been known to walk through the neighborhood, engage people in conversation as they water their lawns or work on their cars, trying to convince them it's time to move. One of those who followed a canvasser's advice was Felix Jankowski. He described what happened:

> This real estate guy kept dropping by the house. He would talk to me when I watered the lawn. He kept telling me that if I didn't sell now the house would be worth less and less money. Like he said next month he would have to offer me a thousand dollars less. He talked about crime, too, and I agreed with him. It's getting pretty bad. I kept thinking about that, and the business of losing money if I should decide to sell in a few years. So one day I invited him in the house, just like he suggested, and we made a deal. I got a pretty good price, so I'm glad I sold.

When a persistent and persuasive salesman is successful in making such a deal, it makes other neighborhood residents more apprehensive and less likely to continue resisting efforts to make them sell. The key point here is how real estate dealers link together two separate but related matters: a fear of crime, and a fear of declining property values.

We have shown how residents have adopted a wait-and-see attitude with regard to the crime situation. Now along comes a salesman telling them things aren't going to get any better, and that they will probably get worse. So it's very likely, the salesman will continue to say, that in the near future you will be forced to move. He argues that the longer you wait, the less chance you have of receiving a good price for your home. That approach can be very convincing. Especially since published statistics showing an increase in the average value of homes in Detroit from 1968 to 1971 do not seem realistic to residents of this neighborhood.[10] For they listen to the purported experts—real estate agents—who tell quite a different story.[11] Furthermore, since this is a closely knit community, people know what their neighbor's homes have sold for. And those figures are indeed declining. For example, the selling price for an average wood-frame house in 1971 was around $12,000. Yet in 1975 two such homes in excellent condition were sold for $7,000 each! Of course, they were purchased by real estate companies, then resold at a profit, but what matters here is the owners received only $7,000. Seemingly, companies prefer to buy the homes themselves, so they, rather than the owners, can reap the benefits. That is why statistics are misleading.

In 1973 a young family contacted a real estate company to handle the sale of their three-bedroom brick home, including a two-car garage. It was appraised by the Federal Housing Administration (FHA) at $19,500. But after months and months, nothing happened. No prospective buyers were shown through the house, it was not advertised in the paper, and the company was generally uncooperative. So the owners called another firm and arranged for them to list the house. Still, there wasn't much action. When a Black family did make a bid, the bank turned down their request for a mortgage (after a three-month period), and the owners were right back where they were six months before.[12] Then came the hustle. The real estate company said they would "solve the problem and help the family out" by purchasing the home—for the incredibly low price of $10,000! After months and months of waiting, and continually hassling with salesmen, the owners agreed, although reluctantly. But they felt they had no other choice, mainly because of the methods used by the real estate dealers.

The problem of declining property values, or more accurately the average sale price of homes in the neighborhood, is intimately related to the purchase of a new or used place in the suburbs. Quite simply, the brick house that sold for $10,000 here would bring at least $30,000 in Warren, and closer to $40,000 in Troy. And parishioners say the suburban homes are not as well constructed, like the man who sold his brick home to an agent:

> If my house was in Troy we would have gotten $35,000. But because it's in the city we got $10,000. And what really makes me angry is that we got real plaster walls, oak floors, and stained glass windows. The suburban homes, especially the newer ones, got

plasterboard walls and plywood floors. But they're not in the city, so they're worth more. So I'm getting ripped off. They'll take my house and sell it for $15,000. Now I'm going to have to get a big mortgage for a house in Warren, a house that is not as good as the one I just sold. And I'll have to work seven days a week, twelve hours a day, just to meet the payments. Two more years and I would have had the old mortgage completely paid off. Now I'm going to be "house poor." But what if I waited? My house would have sold for $10,000, and the one in Warren would have shot up to $40,000. So the longer I wait, the more chance I have of getting screwed. Looks like the wife will have to get a job.

But unlike that St. Thaddeus parishioner, most people are unable to assume the financial risk of moving. So they stay on, continually intimidated by crime, daunted by real estate salesmen, chronically disturbed by the situation. What's more, they feel powerless to change it, to turn around what is happening to their community. But the question is, are parishioners also concerned about Blacks moving into the neighborhood? And the answer, however ambivalent, is Yes and No.

ETHNICITY, SOCIAL CLASS, AND THE URBAN DILEMMA

"You social scientists got it all wrong," argued Maggie Krajewski, an articulate woman who works the afternoon shift at the Mount Elliot Chrysler plant:

You people are all the same. Everybody calls us racists, just because we want to live in a Polish-American neighborhood. I'm sick and tired of hearing all these educated people telling the rest of us how we should live, especially those limousine liberals who live in Grosse Pointe or West Bloomfield, or the middle-class Blacks who live in the city and send their kids to private schools. Hell no, I don't mind if a Black family moves in next door or across the street. Right now there are four Black families on our street and there ain't no problems for anyone. They even send their kids to St. Thaddeus school. But when you ask me if I would be happy with a majority of Blacks in the neighborhood, I would have to say no. Go ahead, call me a racist. I don't give a damn. The reason I feel like I do is this: if we had a majority of Blacks, then this neighborhood

wouldn't be the same anymore. It wouldn't be a Polish neighborhood. Is there something wrong with me feeling that way? According to you educated people, there is. I'm supposed to feel guilty.
Well, I don't! Reading books and getting degrees is supposed to
make people smart. But you people don't know nothing when it
comes to understanding people. You don't know nothing!

In 1970 only 1.6 percent of all neighborhood residents were
Black.[13] But changes have taken place in this "sub-community," a
locale that includes several adjacent census tracts.[14] The Black
population of the sub-community in which the neighborhood is
located increased from 7 percent in 1960 to 14 percent in 1970.[15]
That is due largely to what has taken place in the census tracts to
the immediate north and south of the parish neighborhood. Between 1960 and 1970, the Black population of the northern tract
increased from 10 to 20 percent; to the south, that figure jumped
from 5.9 to 23.1 percent.[16] Thus while the sub-community has
more Blacks than it did ten years ago, the St. Thaddeus neighborhood did not experience a significant change. And parishioners are
pleased about that.

Their concern, as Maggie Krajewski has said, is that the neighborhood will become predominantly Black. And they are fully
aware of the fact that that has happened in other white ethnic
communities throughout the city. They also know how the "self-
fulfilling prophecy" notion works. Again, Maggie explains:

> What happens is this. People get up-tight. They see a few Black
> families moving in and they get scared. "They're going to take over
> our community," people say, "and in a few years there won't be
> none of us left." Ain't that true? Ain't this city becoming mostly
> Black? And where are the leaders? Is anybody trying to look at
> what's happening and say "Hey, you white folks don't have to
> move, we'll guarantee you that the neighborhood will remain fifty-
> fifty." Hell no! Are the real estate people saying that? Is the mayor
> saying that? Are the *Free Press* and *News* saying that? Yeah, we talk
> amongst ourselves. I tell people, I say "Hey, we don't have to move
> when a few Black families move in, we don't have to panic." But
> then a real estate salesman convinces someone to sell, and a neigh-
> bor stops me and says "See? I told you so." So we are fighting a
> losing battle, and we ain't getting no help, not from the pastor, not
> from the mayor, not from anyone.

While the main concern of present residents is that the neighborhood will eventually become predominantly Black, still there are
more immediate issues. For example, a great deal of hostility is
directed at the federal government's Department of Housing and
Urban Development (HUD).

Our rented place was next to a house purchased through HUD.
It was sold to a middle-aged Black woman with four children. Her
primary source of income was welfare payments. Within six
months of taking up residence next door, she dropped over to
complain about a faulty furnace. Despite my lack of knowledge, I
went over to take a look. The problem was indeed serious. It was a
bitterly cold winter, and the old furnace was simply not producing
any heat. Meanwhile, the oven on the gas stove was left open to
supply some warmth in the kitchen, where her children huddled
together under blankets. A plumbing and heating expert was called
in, and after thoroughly examining the furnace, concluded that
the repairs were too costly. "You may as well buy a new one," he
said, "because you're gonna have to pay me a lot to get this one in
working order, and then, because it's so old, I can't guarantee the
job." The woman followed his advice, but that meant it was impossible for her to make house payments for a number of months.
Soon, her furniture and belongings were placed on the sidewalk,
and she was evicted. The next day, three men arrived in a van,
and boarded-up the windows and doors. But teenagers got in
through a basement window and used the vacant house as a meeting place. Two months later we noticed smoke billowing from the
basement and called the fire department. It was too late; by the
time the fire was extinguished, only a partial structure remained.
Now it became an eyesore, and a potential danger to children who
might wander in among the debris. Finally, we convinced officials
that the house should be bulldozed; the wrecking company left an
ugly lot strewn with broken glass, splintered wood, and burnt
timbers. Yet the lending company that held an FHA guaranteed
mortgage was paid in full. So who was the loser? The woman who
purchased the home. She is now living in a relative's apartment, a
small place that houses eight children and two adults. And the
neighborhood residents are still left with an unsightly vacant lot in
their midst.[17]

The above case was discussed by many parishioners. In addition, they continue to talk about other HUD homes in the neighborhood that are bought by unsuspecting Blacks. "For chrissakes," said a Dad's Club member after one of our meetings,

I can't believe the way those goddamn bureaucrats take advantage of Black women on welfare. They sell them houses that are supposed to be in good shape, but they fall apart in a few months. Then the women ain't got no money for repairs, so they're out on their ear. But the rich get richer, the poor get poorer, and we are left with a mess. It's a God-awful shame. That's why those HUD guys better not come around here talking about low-cost housing schemes. I'll take them on a tour of the neighborhood, and they might not be seen again.

People were also irritated about four new homes that were built in the neighborhood as part of a government-funded project. The houses were prefabricated, shaped like boxes, and placed atop a concrete slab. Their very appearance was upsetting to parishioners. Within a few months the houses literally began to fall apart from sloppy construction. And nine months later, three were boarded-up and surrounded by tall weeds. Residents have attempted to convince authorities to remove them, but they remain, dreadfully out of place in an otherwise immaculate neighborhood.

Based on the observed consequences of well-intended but poorly administered federal programs, parishioners are vehemently against such schemes. Nor are they favorably disposed toward having Black neighbors who are forced to rely on governmental assistance. "In order for this neighborhood to stay the same," said one man, "we need people who are not on welfare, people who can afford to make repairs on the house and keep up the property. Colored people who are on food stamps have a tough time doing that, because they have to worry about getting the food on the table." Thus, social class is of primary importance when Polish Americans discuss potential neighborhood residents.

Working-class Blacks are viewed as desirable neighbors, largely because parishioners have had the opportunity to observe their way of life. The general conclusion is that the two groups have a lot in common. A member of the Usher's Club explains:

Yeah, one of those Black families moved in next door. And you know something, the guy works the same shift I do. And he's working seven days, just like me. Jesus, he's a hard worker. Never misses a day. I was leaving for work one day last week, and we said something about the lousy weather. The guy was coughing and blowing his nose something awful. But he climbed in the car and drove off. Said he couldn't afford to take a day off. And then, when he comes home, he's out there until dark working on the lawn. My old lady tells me his wife is always sweeping the sidewalk, washing windows, and stuff like that. And man, their kids behave. When their old lady says something, they jump. It's really something, you know, they ain't no different from us.

So Michael Novak is correct when he suggests that many white Catholics differentiate among Blacks:

Most Catholics, I believe, perceive at least three strata among Blacks. (Among themselves, they also see the same strata.) First are the highly successful and prominent Blacks, from Martin Luther King, Jr., to Senator Edward Brooke, to the Black athletes, professors, singers, actors, and lawyers they see so often in the media (but seldom in real life). Second comes the black middle-class, pious and disciplined and hard working, whom they do see in their neighborhoods or meet in their schools—people very much like themselves. Third comes the Black underclass: that one-fourth or one-third of the Black population that lives in poverty, joblessness, and the widely publicized "tangle of pathologies."[18]

It is that last group working-class Polish Americans object to as potential neighbors. But they express their animosity in terms of social class, not race. "We want working-people," they say, "people who are more like us." Nevertheless, current residents would not be pleased with a predominantly Black neighborhood, even if those homeowners were members of the working-class. Why? Maggie Krajewski answers that question: "It wouldn't be a Polish neighborhood. . . . It wouldn't be the same anymore." Clearly, Polish Americans are more comfortable with members of their own ethnic group. They would prefer their community to remain as we have described it: a network of nuclear families linked together through participation in the parish, common residence, and a shared value system based on ethnicity. It is difficult

to quantify the meaning of community in the social and psychological sense of the word, but to Polish Americans, only the family
is of greater importance. This is why members of that ethnic group
react as strongly as they do to a perceived threat from outsiders.
And those strangers need not only be Blacks.

In recent years Detroit has experienced an influx of Albanian
immigrants, some of whom have settled in a Polish-American
community near St. Thaddeus. It is interesting to note that long-
time residents of that neighborhood are quite upset about what
they term "an invasion." I spoke with several Polish Americans
there in an attempt to understand their point of view. A retired
foundry worker explained:

> In a few years those Albanians are gonna take over this place. Why,
> you go to church on Sunday, and they're all over. They speak this
> strange-sounding language that doesn't sound nothing like Polish,
> and I don't know, they're just different from us Poles. You know,
> some of us have already moved out. It just ain't the same since they
> started moving in. This has been our community for over fifty years
> now, but soon it'll be all over.

While I did not conduct a thorough investigation of that near-by
parish, it was striking to hear Polish Americans react strongly to
members of another white ethnic group. And I am quite certain
that parishioners from St. Thaddeus would have responded similarly had Albanians joined their parish and purchased homes in
the surrounding area.

The same phenomenon has happened in a Polish parish just
south of Hamtramck. There the new immigrants are from Yugo-
slavia. They arrived within the past five years, and are often a
source of irritation to the Poles. Indeed, stereotypes have developed about the Yugoslavs as a gun-toting violence-prone group.
And clearly, they are unwelcome newcomers and a perceived
threat to a predominantly Polish-American community.

It is important to realize, therefore, that what we have described
is not simply a racial issue. It is a struggle over turf, a desire to
maintain a community of values, a pan-human tendency to ask the
question: "Why can't they be like us?"[19] Given that, what about the
future? The parishioners of St. Thaddeus see three alternatives.

First, they say the neighborhood could remain essentially the same: A Polish-American enclave with a small proportion of Black residents. Second is the possibility of a larger number of Blacks, but not a majority. And finally, current residents speculate about an overwhelmingly Black neighborhood, a complete reversal of the present situation.

It is very unlikely that the Black population will continue to be 1.6 percent of the total, the official 1970 figure. An increasing number of Black families have purchased houses here since that time. Furthermore, Polish Americans are selling: In the summer of 1974 there were fifty homes with "for sale" signs on their neatly mowed lawns.[20] For the neighborhood to maintain its current ethnic makeup, Polish Americans must purchase a majority of the homes. There are positive and negative factors affecting that possibility.

We have already discussed how real estate firms engage in "steering" young white couples away from older city neighborhoods. And the fear of crime would certainly make anyone think twice about choosing the area as a place to live. On the other hand, as we pointed out in a previous chapter, St. Thaddeus school will continue to attract families with young children. (It will also act as a powerful force influencing current residents to stay.) So, too, will the vibrant parish and the excellent condition of the homes. The availability of bus transportation and access to expressways are also important assets. But for many prospective homeowners the liabilities present too great a risk. "You think I'm nuts?" asked the recently married son of a parish member as we discussed the pros and cons of buying a home in the neighborhood.

> There ain't no way! I've seen what my parents have gone through with the crime situation, and that's enough to keep me away. Yeah, I can get a little place in good shape for nine grand or so, but when we have a couple of kids and want a bigger place in the suburbs, will I make a profit on selling it? Can you guarantee me that? Hell no! But if I move to Sterling Heights now, and get a place for $30,000, it will sell for $40,000 in five years. And it's safe out there. So we'll struggle for awhile. So what. I'm young, and can work plenty of overtime. We'll make it. And there ain't no risk involved.

Not all young Polish Americans share this young man's attitude, but the majority I talked with do. What's more, neighborhood residents are aware of that and are thus not optimistic about attracting Polish-American homeowners. So they dismiss the first alternative mentioned above, view the second simply as a transitional phase, and are convinced that the neighborhood will become predominantly Black as time goes on.

"I give it twenty years," said a man who has decided to stay:

> Most of us who live here now just can't afford to move, so it'll be a Black and Polish neighborhood until us older folks start dying off. It'll be old Polish people and young Black families. Then, when we die, it will be all over. Oh, the parish will still be standing, and there will be a few of us around. But the gym will probably become a community center, and maybe the city will buy the school, and who knows what they'll do with the nuns' convent. Maybe turn it into an apartment building or something like that.

Although some parishioners argue about the time factor involved, most agree with that prediction. And they are probably right. Forty-two percent of the males in the community are over forty, and the prospect of taking out a twenty or thirty year mortgage at their age is frightening. Nor does a salary of between eight and twelve thousand dollars a year allow for a hefty savings account, or provide the freedom to move if they choose. So in the years to come those who can afford it may move. And those who can't will remain behind. Perhaps what I have described is a Polish-American community that will not exist in twenty or thirty years. Yet things could change.

THE ETHNIC NEIGHBORHOOD AND PUBLIC POLICY

Peter L. Berger and Richard John Neuhaus have described the neighborhood "as a key mediating structure in the reordering of our national life . . . the place of relatively intact and secure existence, protecting us against the disjointed and threatening big world 'out there.' "[21] A mediating structure is viewed as an institution, like the family, church, and voluntary association, "standing between the individual in his private life and the large institutions of public life."[22]

In the past several years social scientists and policy makers have begun to recognize that, to re-discover the neighborhood, if you will. Howard Hallman writes about the need for neighborhood government and various forms of decentralization, as does Milton Kotler.[23] Arthur Naparstek has addressed the problem of devising policies to heighten the responsiveness of urban governmental structures to neighborhood problems through focusing on citizen involvement.[24] As a result of those efforts, and pressure from local community groups, President Gerald Ford signed the *Home Mortgage Disclosure Act* (in 1975) to prevent "red-lining" in urban areas. And in May 1976 there was a White House conference on "Ethnicity and Neighborhood." Following that, President Ford established The Committee on Urban Development and Neighborhood Revitalization. Also in 1976, The National Neighborhood Policy Act was passed by the Senate to establish a "commission to investigate the factors contributing to the decline of urban neighborhoods and the factors necessary to neighborhood survival and revitalization."[25] While that act did not come up for a vote in the House of Representatives, there is clearly a renewed interest in neighborhood issues at the highest levels of government.

President Jimmy Carter demonstrated his administration's concern when he appointed Msgr. Geno Baroni (whom *The New York Times* referred to "as perhaps the leading champion of the revitalization of the Italian, Polish, Irish, and other ethnic neighborhoods that once so enlivened American cities,") as Assistant Secretary of Housing and Urban Development for Neighborhoods, Nongovernmental Organizations, and Consumer Protection.[26]

It is too soon to tell what effect all of that will have on St. Thaddeus. The government bureaucracy moves slowly and the new interest in neighborhoods is not universally accepted as an appropriate focus of concern. Perhaps the major stumbling block is the reaction noted by Berger and Neuhaus:

> As is evident in fears and confusions surrounding such phrases as "ethnic purity" or neighborhood integrity, the focus on neighborhood touches on some of the most urgent and sensitive issues of social policy. Indeed, many charge that the "rediscovery" of the neighborhood is but another, and thinly veiled, manifestation of racism.[27]

Hopefully, that should not deter us from dealing with the kinds of problems that affect the Polish-American community we have described. Crime is a major concern; real estate firms that engage in "steering," "blockbusting," and general "panic-peddling" do affect the residential patterns of ethnic groups; and Polish Americans do prefer to live in their own neighborhoods. Are we to dismiss their fears as irrational? Will we allow questionable real estate practices to continue? And how do we answer Maggie Krajewski, who asks: "Is there something wrong with me wanting to live in a Polish neighborhood?"

Once those questions are answered we can proceed to follow the advice of Richard Krickus and Stephen Adubato, who recommend "an authentic urban policy which is adequately funded and properly emphasizes residential neighborhoods, for their survival will contribute to the welfare of all people who live in our nation's troubled cities."[28] The people of St. Thaddeus would appreciate such an approach. For they really don't want to move.

Conclusion 7

Polish Americans have been utilized as convenient subjects for the study of social disorganization and the process of assimilation. William I. Thomas was "curious" about their behavior in Chicago saloons, and puzzled by a way of life he termed "incomprehensible."[1] Neil Sandberg and others set out to discover whether members of this ethnic group were more "Polish" or "American."[2] Consequently, in the late 1970s, we know very little about the nature of communal life among Polish Americans. Yet ethnicity remains strong in our social, economic, and political life. And cultural differences persist, even if they appear to go unrecognized by many, including educators, intellectuals, the media, and public-policy makers.

Mindful of what we ought to know about our ethnic groups and convinced that prior studies of Polish Americans did not yield adequate data, I concluded that a substantially different approach was necessary. Based on participant observation and in-depth interviews, I have attempted to portray a contemporary Polish-American community, to focus on the private sphere of life—in the family, the parish, and the neighborhood.

Seventy years after Israel Zangwill's drama *The Melting Pot* was produced on an American stage, we are discussing a vibrant Polish-American community in one of our major cities.[3] If that seems incongruous, we should keep in mind that Zangwill was a playwright, not a prophet. Still, throughout the American historical experience we have witnessed a pervasive attachment to an ideology of assimilation. Given that orientation, it is indeed remarkable to learn that powerful bonds of ethnic communality continue to persist.

145

These bonds have been sustained in this subject community largely because a Roman Catholic parish serves as a source of social organization in an urban neighborhood. St. Thaddeus performs religious functions, like any other parish, but from a strictly sociological point of view the web of relationships formed among its members is of major importance. A social network links nuclear families together so that no parishioner remains a stranger, and so that a neighborhood becomes a community, an identifiable geographic and social unit.

At a time when observers of American life are discussing the decline of the family and predicting its eventual demise, we have found compelling evidence to the contrary. In this sociocultural milieu, the family is a prominent institution. To working-class Polish Americans, nothing is more important. Although a degree of social distance is maintained among nuclear families, and socializing in the home is infrequent, they are not isolated from friends, neighbors, and relatives. Parents and children do participate in the social and organizational life of the parish. Still, the family is an autonomous unit, and privacy is highly valued and carefully maintained. The family, therefore, is a haven, a refuge from the larger society, a source of warmth and affection, a set of relationships in which individuals invest themselves.

Both husbands and wives are devoted to providing their children with the necessities of daily life, and opportunities for success in the future. But social mobility for sons and daughters is not the only factor motivating parents. They want respect and dignity for their children, and they know from their own experience that it must be earned. Polish Americans are fully aware of the vicious stereotypes their group is subjected to. They also know, as members of the working class, that earning a living by working with your hands is devalued and considered a sign of low intelligence by those of higher social status. Furthermore, parents feel there is little hope of an attitudinal change toward their generation. So, for them, children *are* the future: sons and daughters, if they get to go to college, and study hard, may find a job to be proud of; then they will prove, the parents say, that Polish Americans are indeed competent and intelligent.

Mothers and fathers sacrifice for their children and expect them, in turn, to demonstrate that the results were worth the effort. That is one reason why discipline is strict both in the home and the classrooms of the parish school. Parental expectations regarding occupational roles is another factor. But what a mother and father know about jobs in the blue-collar world does not coincide with the requirements of an executive or professional position. So children who are raised with an emphasis on being obedient find it necessary to adjust in order to be successful in the white-collar world.

For parents, sacrificing so that their children may succeed is a risk. In our society, social mobility for members of the working class involves an ironic set of behavior patterns within the family. Mothers and fathers are asked to raise children to become unlike themselves, to proffer their own lives as a warning, not a model.[4] Children who do become successful as far as the larger society is concerned may look down on their parents and reject their own cultural heritage. And youngsters who leave school to work in a factory may disappoint their parents. Thus, sacrificing for the children is an emotional investment that does not always pay off. But family life does have its rewards, and not only when children achieve success in the outside world and maintain a mutually satisfying relationship with their parents.

For we have shown that a husband and wife communicate; they do reveal their personal thoughts and feelings to one another. The stereotypical image of a working-class Polish-American male as a beer-drinking authoritarian who dominates his wife and children has no basis in reality. Nor does the assumption that women are passive and completely dependent on their husbands. In truth, the man of the subject community comes directly home from work because he prefers to spend time with his family. And the marital relationship is quite egalitarian, with a flexible division of labor. A woman shares her husband's trials and tribulations in the workaday world and plans with him for the future. She is, as a mother, a source of emotional support and guidance, a tower of strength. But she does have her own life, close friends with whom intimacies are shared, and the parish, where she is regarded as a competent organizer, a tireless worker, and a strong leader. Yet for both husband and wife, the most meaningful thing in their lives is the family.

Like a nuclear family, an ethnic parish is a "mediating structure."[5] It is another institution standing as a buffer between individuals and the larger society. Indeed, with a church, a school,
and fifteen organizations, St. Thaddeus is a sub-society based on
ethnicity, religion, and common residence. It provides parishioners with the opportunity to participate, both religiously and
socially, in an environment that is comforting and supportive.
Changes in the church may be difficult to accept, but the Catholic
religion remains a guiding light, a way of ordering one's life.
Despite new forms of worship and the disappearance of some
familiar rituals and symbols, a parish member can still go to confession and hear mass in Polish. Thus while Catholicism is changing, it has not become less important in the lives of working-class
Polish Americans.

If religion is the means to eternal salvation, then parish organizational and social life is a way of enjoying the present as it
unfolds to that end. Men, women, and children are involved in
clubs that sponsor a wide variety of events and activities to support
the church, school, and athletic program. There is the Madonna
Guild for women, the Dad's Club for men, a cub scout group for
youngsters, and a recently formed association for senior citizens.
Bingo is a weekly affair, and every year there is a Christmas party,
a Mardi Gras dance, and a polka party. Those are just a few of the
organizations and social events at St. Thaddeus, but they show
that the parish performs an important social function by providing
a opportunity for Polish Americans to interact with one another.
As a result of that interaction, linkages among nuclear families are
established and maintained, and an ethnic community is formed
and sustained.

But parishioners are worried about the future of this community. Their fears are symbolized by a desperate struggle to keep the
St. Thaddeus school open in the face of powerful economic, political, and social forces. With a decline in the number of teaching
nuns, the parish has had to hire lay teachers at higher wages.
Furthermore, while operating costs have spiralled in an inflation-
ary economy, there are fewer students and thus less income from
tuition payments. In the past few years the school has depended on
proceeds from the annual parish festival to meet its expenses, but a

portion of what is earned at that event must be turned over to the Archdiocese of Detroit. Here is where simple economics becomes complicated by political and social factors. For the archdiocese provides financial assistance to inner-city Black parishes, including support for schools. The parishioners of St. Thaddeus resent that. They are aware Black parishes have financial problems, and support their right to receive aid. Their argument, however, is that the problems of St. Thaddeus seem to go unrecognized by members of the church hierarchy in Detroit. Parishioners say, "We need help too; we have to put on a festival to raise money for the school, so why can't we keep what we earn?"

This issue has never been adequately addressed as far as the members of St. Thaddeus are concerned. Consequently, they remain hostile toward the archdiocese and the Black parishes it supports. Presently, then, two ethnic groups who share the same city and face similar problems are inadvertently pitted against one another by the policies and programs of a larger institution. And that serves to show what can happen when well-intentioned people fail to realize that *both* Blacks and white ethnics have unmet needs.

Let us return to our discussion of St. Thaddeus school for a moment. The fact that children receive a Catholic education there is only one reason parishioners feel strongly about keeping its doors open. Many believe the future of this Polish-American community is dependent on what happens to the school in the years to come. If it remains open, people argue, current residents with children will stay, and the neighborhood will attract young Polish-American families. But if the school closes, parents will move to the suburbs, where their children can get a Catholic education, and the neighborhood will lose its appeal for Polish Americans with school-age youngsters. Eventually, parishioners say, that would result in a predominantly Black neighborhood. Such a prospect is not pleasing to the Polish Americans who live there now. That is why St. Thaddeus school has become something more than an educational institution; it is seen as the key to maintaining this urban ethnic community. But other factors are also important.

Violence and crime in the neighborhood have frightened residents and altered their patterns of behavior. Vacations are post-poned indefinitely, and a trip to the corner store has become a hazardous journey. Parents are anxious about the safety of their children, and are cautious about where and when the youngsters play. Senior citizens pass up a club meeting or a bingo night for fear of being mugged, and protect their homes with dead-bolt locks and prayers. But these preventative measures seem to be of little help, so some sell their homes and leave.

That pleases panic-peddling real estate dealers who spend a great deal of time and effort attempting to convince other home-owners to do the same. Through phone calls, handbills, and walks through the neighborhood, persistent and persuasive real estate salesmen ply their trade. "You ought to sell now," they say, "and it's best if you sell to us. We can give you cash and save you the hassle of waiting until a buyer comes along." But while sellers may save time, they lose money. For an agency is willing to purchase a home for cash so that a tidy profit can be made on reselling it.

Steering is another practice engaged in by salesmen. Young white families are subtly encouraged not to buy homes in the neighborhood, but to move to the suburbs. And Blacks are steered away from Sterling Heights or Troy for sections of Detroit like the St. Thaddeus area. Such questionable approaches do affect the residential patterns of ethnic groups in the city and the metropoli-tan area. And they exacerbate racial tensions.

The public policy implications of neighborhood issues are both urgent and sensitive. And while there is no clear course of action which solves all the problems we have outlined, some suggestions and recommendations may be helpful.

Crime in our cities must be recognized as both effect and cause. It is a manifestation of societal inequality, of poverty and unem-ployment, of inadequate education, of a lack of opportunities. Those conditions need to be changed. Black youth who turn to crime in Detroit and other cities must be given the opportunity to acquire skills and earn a decent living through a job that is both meaningful and satisfying. In addressing the problem of how soci-ety affects lower-class Black life, Elliot Liebow has given us some advice that is relevant here:

For many Negro men, jobs are no longer enough. Before he can earn a living, he must believe that he can do so, and his women and children must learn to believe this along with him. But he finds it difficult to begin without their support, and they find it difficult to give their support until he begins. The beginning, then, will doubtless be a slow one, but, once started, success will feed on itself just as failure has done. A beginning must be made, however, and it must be made simultaneously at all points in the life cycle. Children and young people must have good schools and good teachers who can give them the skills and the training to compete for jobs and careers, and they must have teachers to believe in them and help them believe in themselves. Jobs that pay enough to support a family must be opened up to the adult generation so they can support their families, so that the young people can see the changed reality, so that young and old can experience it and gain a vested interest in the world they live in.[6]

But in addition to dealing with the problems that make crime an effect, we must realize that crime, in and of itself, is also a cause. We need not repeat here the havoc it has wreaked in an urban Polish-American neighborhood, as well as the larger city. We do need to emphasize, however, that corrective measures are in order. Detroit's neighborhood-based "mini-police stations" have not had a major impact on reducing crime and violence, so other approaches should be planned, implemented, and evaluated. Residents would prefer to see policemen "pounding a beat." Doubtless, that could be expensive for any city. Yet upper middle-class neighborhoods have hired their own police force to insure the safety and security of their living space. Are less affluent families to be denied similar protection because they can't afford it? It certainly seems that way. But until crime is dealt with realistically, with a clarity of purpose and an innovative approach, people will continue to leave the city, or wish that they could.

Some efforts have already been made to alter what are questionable and perhaps illegal real estate practices. But nothing short of an intensive and in-depth inquiry into the methods of urban real estate salesmen and their agencies will uncover the depth of the problems and point the way toward practical and effective solutions. Making a profit is the American way of life. Yet when urban malaise becomes a profitable enterprise, it is time for public-policy makers to be seriously concerned about why that has happened and how it can be stopped as well as prevented.

The more complex and sensitive issue is what Milton Gordon has called "the built-in tension between the goals of ethnic communality and desegregation."[7] We have shown that the parishioners of St. Thaddeus want their community to remain predominantly Polish-American. We have also pointed out how such a preference is viewed by the larger society as irrational racism. While that conclusion is misleading, arguments for preserving ethnic communality and a distinct sub-culture do clash with the democratic ideal that every American should be free to live wherever he pleases. Yet this perplexing problem will not be solved by dismissing the concerns of one group and being attentive to another. Gordon is correct when he argues that "ethnic communality . . . is a powerful force in American life."[8] So it is not incompatible with American history and tradition to ask whether our ideals are achieved by interfering with the personal decisions of Polish Americans who prefer to live in a sociocultural milieu where primary group relations with members of one's own ethnic group are the order of the day. We must also be mindful of the findings of this study that show that working-class Polish Americans are not against having Black neighbors, which is contrary to what many observers believe. The major problem is to devise policies that retain ethnic communality and promote integration rather than resegregation—the prevailing pattern in most urban neighborhoods. Blacks and Poles can live together in harmony, but so far they have been deprived of the opportunity to prove it.

I began this study by saying it was not my attempt to develop generalizations about Polish-American communal life. In fact, a lack of data from other communities makes that impossible. But I would like to comment on an apparent trend to view the working class as a homogenous group with a similar way of life. Doubtless there are similarities. Yet the structure of a working-class Polish-American community is very different from that of an Italian-American neighborhood in Boston. The former is based on a parish, the latter, what Herbert Gans has called "the peer group society."[9] Furthermore, there are striking differences between the nature of the marital relationship in the two groups.

Nor do the Polish Americans I have described compare in all respects to the West Coast families studied by Lillian Breslow Rubin.[10] In some ways, they are alike. But ethnicity and religion do not appear to be significant influences on the lives of blue-collar workers in the San Francisco Bay area. And one wonders just how important the community is.

All in all then, we need more ethnographies dealing with social class and ethnicity. Only then will we begin to appreciate and understand the truly diverse society in which we live.

Epilogue

The first public reading based on this study and its major conclusions generated a storm of controversy which lasted for two months. The anger, confusion, and misunderstandings point up the problems of all ethnic groups—how they see themselves, how others see them, and how the media can distort and reinforce these images.

I was asked to participate in a symposium on "Work in America," to be held at the 1976 annual meeting of the American Association for the Advancement of Science (AAAS). I accepted the invitation and chose to speak on "Polish-American Men: As Workers, As Husbands, and As Fathers."

All participants were advised to arrive in Boston on February 21, the day before the scheduled symposium, to take part in a brief press conference. We were asked to bring with us ten copies of our presentation for distribution to the news media. I arrived early that morning, deposited the copies of my nine-page paper with the AAAS press office, and went for a long walk. When I returned, minutes before the scheduled press conference, I found it difficult to maneuver my way through the crowds of newspaper reporters and TV crews. Perhaps ten to fifteen rooms on one floor had been reserved for media coverage of the annual meeting. Teletype machines chattered away in one room, a bearded scientist faced TV cameras and bright lights in a second room, and twenty-five reporters typed furiously in another to meet their deadlines. I had attended many professional meetings, but never had I witnessed a similar scene. It was a good introduction to the culture of the news media. But that was just the beginning.

The press conference was held in a large room with about eighty

155

to a hundred reporters present. Each symposium participant got up
and summarized his or her paper in five minutes. My statement
was very brief. I said that Polish-American men had not been the
subject of many studies, and that after sixteen months of living in
a working-class Polish-American community, I found them very
much aware of prevailing stereotypes about blue-collar workers
and members of their ethnic group. I talked about "the hidden
injuries of class," and suggested that low self-esteem was an inevitable result of the larger society's negative attitudes toward Polish-
American blue-collar workers.[1]

After the conference I was approached by a *Detroit Free Press*
reporter who requested an interview. I saw no harm, and agreed.
We chatted briefly about my own background; then she requested
a copy of the paper, which I gave her. I then went to meet with a
sociologist from Poland who was completing her doctoral dissertation on Boston's Polonia.

I told her about the press conference and the interview, and she
became visibly agitated and pale. "You have no idea of what
you're in for," she said. "The newspapers will distort your findings, the Polish-American community will be in an uproar,
and . . . and . . . let me see exactly what you've written, right
now!" As she turned the pages, underlined key sentences, and
commented to herself in Polish, I began to feel apprehensive. "I
know what you're trying to say," she remarked quietly upon reading the last page, "but you've made a poor choice of words for a
lay audience, and given the media coverage of this conference,
that's who will read this stuff." She continued,

> Let me tell you something. Last year a magazine with a large
> national distribution reported on a study I co-authored with a col-
> league.[2] It was a survey of the literature on Polish Americans, and
> meant for academicians. But a few quotes were picked up out of
> context, and people thought *I* was calling Polish Americans "back-
> ward, clumsy, and ignorant." When what we were trying to do was
> show how *society* perpetuates those stereotypes and negative images.
> At any rate, all hell broke loose here in Boston's Polish-American
> community, and no matter how I try to explain myself, many
> people continue to believe I'm basically trying to harm Polish-
> Americans.

"Here, look at the sentences I've underlined in your paper," she said. I flipped through the pages and read what I had written in a new light:

Generally speaking, the men in this community view themselves as unintelligent factory workers unworthy of respect and incapable of accomplishing anything worthwhile except supporting a family through hard work and the ability to sacrifice.

Women view a man's attitude towards work as the most important factor to consider in choosing a future husband.

When marital problems arise the general belief is that it is best to suffer through the experience rather than seek professional help.

But perhaps the most striking finding that applies to both husbands and wives in this community is that their lives are centered on the children. Indeed, at times it is as if men and women exist not as individuals in their own right, but as mothers and fathers whose primary role in life is sacrificing for the sake of their children.

Polish-American men in this community have one major goal with regard to their role as parents: to raise children whose lives will be significantly different from their own.

While there's nothing wrong with hard work, there is something very wrong with a society that says who you are is based on what you do for a living; there is something very wrong with a society which uses the color of a man's collar as a measure of his intelligence. In America a man is considered unintelligent if he operates a drill press in a factory. And he is considered stolid and dull if he is a Polish American. The men in the community I studied are fully aware of what society says about them. It is tragic that so many believe it.

All of those statements could easily be misinterpreted or taken out of context. Furthermore, in my attempt to convince scientists how societal attitudes affect individuals, perhaps I overemphasized the degree to which low self-esteem is a problem among working-class Polish-American males. The first and last sentences underlined by my colleague certainly seemed to suggest that possibility. What's more, I thought, how would college faculty members react if an anthropologist said they had a poor self-image because they were reading books on transactional analysis, joining encounter groups, and grappling with identity crises? Doubtless I was dealing with a very sensitive issue. But for now, the die was cast. I thanked my Polish friend and headed for the press room to arrange an appointment with the *Free Press* reporter.

We met the next morning, three hours before the start of the symposium. I stated my concern that a news article would be misinterpreted, and explained that my paper was meant for an audience of social scientists. I also mentioned that the brief presentation was based on a lengthy community study and therefore only a partial picture of the way of life among working-class Polish Americans. The reporter suggested I call a *Free Press* editor to express my point of view. I did, and the editor said she would see to it that the *Free Press* story dealt with my concerns. Indeed, I was told the newspaper was aware of the potential difficulties involved, and planned to include in their report a sentence that clearly stated the researcher *was not* saying Polish Americans were stolid and dull. "Nevertheless," the editor said, "it is a good story, and since the wire services have now picked it up, we have no alternative but to run our first-hand account of your presentation."

Now it was time for the symposium to begin. It took me less than fifteen minutes to read my paper to an attentive audience that had no idea of what had been happening behind the scenes. But while I was responding to questions from the floor, a member of the AAAS media liaison team walked into the room and informed me that a group of reporters was eagerly waiting to meet with me. My paper was "the talk of the press corps," and additional copies were being made as quickly as possible. While less than pleased with that turn of events, I thought a meeting with reporters might provide an opportunity to explain my point of view more fully.

In the press room I was introduced to writers from *The New York Times, The San Francisco Chronicle,* and seven other newspapers from across the country. "We heard about your paper," one of them said, "and we think it's a great story. Do you care to elaborate on what you said?" I stressed several major points and emphasized that it was important not to take things out of context, to realize that my intent was to show how negative stereotypes about blue-collar Polish-Americans are pernicious and need to be eliminated from the contemporary American scene. Actually, the reporters asked very few questions. They immediately sat down at their typewriters, their notes on the interview and a copy of my paper flanking both sides of the machines, and proceeded to write their stories.

I checked out of the hotel and hailed a taxi. As luck would have it, I shared the ride to the airport with one of the reporters who had interviewed me, and I asked him why my paper had attracted so much attention among the press corps. "There are several reasons," the veteran journalist said:

> First of all, our newspapers send us here to come back with a story that will appeal to our readers. So we attend all the press briefings and read a lot of papers. At a conference like this one, there are many physical scientists dealing with subjects we know little about. Furthermore, their papers are filled with jargon and poorly written. So we have a difficult time trying to figure out what they're trying to say. And we know if we have trouble, our report probably won't be a good story for lay readers. So we look for papers about people, like yours, for example. It was brief, easy to understand, filled with "good" quotes that make a story appealing, and to the point. In short, we could read it and easily file a good story with no sweat. Also, we all knew about your conversation with the *Free Press* reporter. And that immediately sparked our interest. Hell, that was a story in itself.

"What about the fact that I was talking about blue-collar Polish Americans," I asked. "Was that a factor?"

"Hell, yes," he answered, "they're people, and our publishers know they can sell papers with stories about people, especially those who live in our urban centers. And if the story is a controversial one, so much the better."

The next morning's *Washington Post* carried an article headlined "The Polish Stereotype," in which Thomas O'Toole informed readers that

> most of the men [I studied] had dropped out of high school for blue-collar jobs, which they regard as the only thing they can do. They dismiss their workaday lives as little more than a means of earning enough money to support families. Their whole goal life [sic] is to send their children to college so they won't be like them.

"Me?" one man told Wrobel, "I just work in a factory, nothing special. Same old thing day after day now for 20 years. But it pays the bills. So I can't complain."

None of them complain about their status, Wrobel said. In fact, they wonder why anybody complains about status in life.

"All I expect is decent pay for hard work," another man said in what Wrobel called a typical attitude. "Now it's gettin' so that young kids and black folks are always asking for more and more benefits. What the hell do they expect? Something for nothing?"

The men's wives do little to help the men feel differently, Wrobel said. Their first concern about their husbands is how hard they are willing to work.

Many of the marriages Wrobel observed were unhappy, but the men and women all endured them even though they said they believed in divorce.[3]

Those are excerpts from O'Toole's story. I compared them with what I had written. Yes, his quotes *were* my quotes, exactly as they appeared in the AAAS paper. But I had not said that the men had quit school. What I did mention was the median educational level in the community. Yes, I did point out that wives felt it was important to choose husbands who were willing to work hard, but I did not suggest that their point of view implied, or could be interpreted to mean, that a woman was unsupportive toward her spouse. Yet O'Toole's statement—"The men's wives do little to help them feel differently"—certainly gave that impression. Furthermore, nowhere did I suggest or imply that "many of the marriages were unhappy." But O'Toole's even more serious error was in what he failed to say. There was no reference in his article to my analysis of the relationship between societal attitudes and personal feelings. Therefore, the readers could easily conclude that I was "blaming the victim."

That same day, related stories were carried in The Detroit News and The Detroit Free Press. On the front page of the News, captioned "Detroit Poles Feel They're Unworthy, Study Discloses," was the O'Toole article, word for word, reprinted from the Post wire service.[4] Its continuation on page five was captioned "Poles seen self-demeaning."

The *Free Press* ran a story on page three, its so-called second front page. The headline was "Study Finds Bad Polish Image."[5] But, as the editor had promised, the report was accurate, especially in comparison to O'Toole's, which the *News* picked up without ever contacting me for confirmation or elaboration. Furthermore, the *Free Press* story included the following paragraphs:

> Wrobel said he is concerned that his findings may be misinterpreted and that some people may think he is implying that Polish people are not intelligent. He emphasized that these findings are about Polish Americans' image of themselves, not about their actual intelligence.
>
> In fact, he pointed out, a majority of the men in his community are intelligent and highly skilled craftsmen who happen to have a poor image of themselves. As in any community, the people in his community possess a wide range of skills and intelligence levels, he said.[6]

The report concluded with a discussion of how societal attitudes toward blue-collar workers and Polish Americans were responsible for the feelings I had described. That was encouraging. But then I called my secretary from the Merrill-Palmer Institute, a highly efficient and sensitive second-generation Polish-American woman who had just recently been assigned to my office, and who had typed the paper I presented in Boston.

She had spent the entire day handling irate callers. Perhaps thirty-five individuals had phoned, she said, all of whom were Polish Americans:

> I tried to explain what you were trying to say. I spoke Polish and told them you meant no harm. I even read them portions of the presentation that had not been quoted in the newspapers; but, Paul, people are angry, very angry, and I don't think they listened to me. What are we going to do?

I didn't know; what's more, now I felt badly that she was placed in the position of defending me.

Then, five parishioners from St. Thaddeus, those we knew best, came to my house to discuss the situation. They were very supportive. "You know," one woman said, "we all read your dissertation. You probably forgot you asked us to read a rough draft before you sent it off to the university. So, remember, we all know what you said and what you were trying to do. Those newspapers don't tell the whole story, and those headlines, why they're just ridiculous." Her husband asked if I had seen the 6:00 P.M. news on TV. I hadn't, but it was now time for the 11:00 P.M. broadcast, so we turned on the TV and waited.

Soon, the anchorman said a local anthropologist had studied a Detroit Polish-American community and found that the men thought they were unintelligent. To get reactions to those findings, the TV station had sent a film crew to Hamtramck, a predominantly Polish-American city located within the boundaries of Detroit, to interview people "on the street." We saw a reporter thrust his microphone in the face of a Polish-American teenager and ask something like: "Do you agree with Dr. Wrobel's findings that Polish Americans feel unintelligent? Do *you* feel unintelligent?" The boy was puzzled, but he disagreed with "my findings" as quickly as he could, and headed off down the street.

We were appalled. We thought of calling our own press conference to straighten things out, but finally decided it might only make things worse. After all, I had used a pseudonym for the parish, and once reporters knew where it was they might annoy the parishioners and disrupt their daily lives. Then, too, a press conference would create a "better story," and that would serve to focus attention away from the real issues. So we decided to wait and see what would happen.

The next two days both Detroit newspapers carried stories describing reactions to their initial coverage of my AAAS presentation. Some of the captions were, "Detroit Poles Attack Study on Self-Image" and "Poles in Detroit Reject Bad Image in Study."[7] I also learned that over thirty-five newspapers across the country had reported on my research. Phone calls and letters were coming in from Chicago, Philadelphia, Buffalo, Rochester, Minneapolis, and even Los Angeles, St. Petersburg, and Bangor, Maine. *The Chicago Sun-Times* wrote about the responses of that city's Polish Americans, under the caption "Ethnic Study Stirs Strong Reaction," and later published an editorial entitled "Ethnic Self-Image: No Joke."[8] Other newspapers followed in the same pattern. But none of them printed as many letters to the editor as *The Detroit*

News. Twelve days after my Boston presentation, they continued to publish angry letters. Here are excerpts from several:

March 1, 1976

It was a waste of money and sacrifice for Dr. Wrobel's parents to send him to college. No anthropologist worthy of the name would confine a study to so small a group.

I worked 30 years in a small factory to help my family. There is nothing wrong with working overtime and saving some money! I also found time for relatives and friends, good times and vacations—and for night school to improve myself. I am Polish and proud of it.

Your story was misleading. The survey painted a picture of Poles as little more than ignorant, complacent laborers who are ashamed of themselves and their country.

March 6, 1976

This is in protest of Dr. Paul Wrobel's so-called survey of the Polish people you ran a story on. I am Polish and proud of it. I reared three boys and all have master's degrees. I think Wrobel is the "dumb Polack" for conducting such a survey, which was not representative at all.

Numbers of us, who are or were extensively involved in Polish affairs, cannot accept the ultimate conclusion addressed to Poles as "unworthy," "stolid and dull." Constructive criticism is always welcome and beneficial but a study with some unprobable results, doubtful research methods, and suspicion of bias, can only mislead the readers and perform unnecessary harm to the parties involved.

Our father is a second-generation Pole who worked hard and sacrificed much for his family. At 69, he's still at it. He rises at 5 A.M. and drives 80 miles to Brighton, where he is a blue-collar employee of a tool and die shop. He endures many ethnic jokes but is proud of his Polish heritage and equally proud to be an American.

March 9, 1976

Wrobel labeled Poles as "unworthy" and said they are "incapable of anything worthwhile except supporting a family through hard work." Yet Wrobel concluded that a Polish-American father is "a husband, a father, a factory worker, a Roman Catholic, a parish member and a homeowner concerned about maintaining the safety of his home and the security of his family." Are they unworthy then? What a strange conclusion.

I am Polish and proud! My father was someone to look up to, a proud metal finisher at Fisher Body. We lived through the Depression and never were on welfare—and he educated five of us in parochial schools. Surely all fathers feel the same way, loving their families and doing their best for them. We were taught love, respect, courtesy, industriousness, the value of money, the value of our religion—and most of all, to be proud of our Polish heritage. I resent Wrobel's study depicting Poles as stupid and dull. It wasn't at all representative. I wouldn't attempt to write a thesis unless I first knew what I was writing about. That's where Wrobel wobbled. He sure missed the boat.

In response to such letters I drafted an explanation of why I wrote the nine-page paper and described what I had tried to say. It was published in both Detroit newspapers.[9] I also informed readers that I had earlier taped a TV show dealing with my study, as part of Wayne State University course on "Work and Society," and provided the date and time the program would be aired.

To respond to critics in other cities I sent copies of my Boston presentation to Polish-American leaders and spent hours on the phone with callers who wanted to speak with me in person. Some were so angry they would start swearing at whoever picked up the phone, and we received several threats of violence.

While responding to critics absorbed a great deal of my time, I was also busy contending with representatives of the media who were requesting interviews and inviting me to be a guest on television talk shows. Given the nature of the publicity so far, and the way newspapers continued to play up the matter, I was reluctant to be interviewed for fear of making the situation worse. When reporters called, I got the feeling they were more interested in a sensational story than an accurate explanation. Furthermore, I was put off by the persistence and seemingly arrogant attitude of some, who even argued that I "owed" them an interview. Then, there were two who went to further lengths. A young woman reporter called from a suburban newspaper and pleaded with me that she was on probation, that her future was in my hands. For if I agreed to an interview, she said, her boss would have no doubts about her ability as a top-notch investigative reporter. Another female journalist asked if we could meet for a late dinner in a quiet place, then perhaps return to her apartment where we could chat in a private place, have a few drinks, and "really get to know each other, as a man and woman do." In both cases, I demurred.

With regard to television appearances, the issue was quite different. I wanted what I considered an adequate amount of time to explain what I had written. But TV stations could not guarantee that. Barbara Walters's office called with regard to a possible appearance on the "Today" program, and I thought that would be an excellent opportunity to reach a national audience and clear up some of the confusion surrounding my study. But the person to whom I spoke said she had no way of knowing just how long I'd be on camera. "It might be four minutes," she said, "or it could be 45 seconds." That was unacceptable, as were the offers from local stations, so I decided to forget about television. But what happened next made that impossible.

An NBC field producer, working out of Chicago, called and asked if he could film an interview with me for a segment on the network's daily evening news program. He said that he was putting together a story on Polish Americans in Detroit and Chicago, and would very likely get a three or four minute segment of the nightly news. Four minutes to cover Detroit *and* Chicago meant I would have only a few seconds. I mentioned that problem to the producer, but he argued that several seconds on national TV is a lifetime to those who work in the industry. It wasn't enough for me, and I said as much. The producer told me he was on the way to Detroit anyhow, with a film crew, and would call later to see if I had changed my mind.

The next day, I received a call from a Polish-American colleague. He had seen an NBC film crew in a Hamtramck bar. Someone from the team had asked the Polish Americans present to line up against the wall, drinks in hand, and sing a Polish song. Then, the cameras started rolling. My friend was incensed. "Can you imagine how that would look on national TV?" he asked. "What the hell are those characters doing here anyhow, and what right do they have to stage a scene like that? Why, that film will just serve to reinforce existing stereotypes." I agreed, and told him of my conversation with the field producer.

That same afternoon the NBC producer called again. "Guess where I am," he said. I had no idea, and told him to quit playing games. "Well," he said with a sarcastic chuckle, "would you believe I'm in the St. Thaddeus rectory? We've been doing some filming around here, you know, of the school children playing, the church, and we got some people to talk to us. Now we'd like to come down to interview you."

I was angry. Every reporter I had spoken to, from both local and national newspapers, had honored my request to retain the anonymity of the parish. When I began the study I promised the pastor and parishioners that no names would be revealed, including the name of the parish. Everyone seemed pleased with that arrangement, for, as I explained earlier, privacy is highly valued. Now it was threatened by a national TV network.

I expressed my concerns to the producer as calmly as I could, but did mention that there appeared to be a legal question involved. After all, I had used a pseudonym for a purpose, and he was deliberately ignoring my, as well as the community's, wishes. I asked how he found out the name and location of the parish. "I'm sorry," he replied, "I cannot reveal my sources."

The lawyer I contacted said there was nothing I could do. One can't assume to protect the privacy of others, he told me. So if a reporter got permission to film on parish property, that was that. I called the rectory to speak to Fr. Bulakowski, who had been a great help so far, and who was also wary of any further publicity. But it was his day off, and the regular parish secretary was home sick. Her replacement had agreed to the filming without thinking of the possible consequences. Not seeing any alternative, I phoned the producer and told him we could meet that evening for an off-the-record talk. By now, other Polish Americans in Detroit were aware of what was happening, and several called to complain. "Now what are you getting us into?" one asked. I didn't know. Nor did I trust the NBC producer. So I asked a friend to join me for our evening meeting.

We introduced ourselves and sipped coffee. My colleague and I expressed our displeasure with the staged bar scene and the filming at St. Thaddeus. Our host listened to our objections, but argued that he saw nothing wrong with either ploy. Furthermore, he repeated that he wanted to film an interview with me, especially because I was so "controversial." I restated my feelings on the matter and thought it would be dropped once and for all. But then he said:

> You and your friend here don't like the idea that I filmed Poles in a bar, while they were singing and drinking beer, and you're also concerned about maintaining the anonymity of St. Thaddeus. Well, I'll tell you, I don't want you guys to get the idea I'm blackmailing you or anything like that, because that's the furthest thing from my mind, but I'll tell you what. Dr. Wrobel, if you agree to be interviewed I can promise you that I will not use any of the film I took in the bar or at the parish.

Needless to say, my friend and I were shocked. And now there was no way I would consent to be interviewed. We left, wondering if there was anything we could do about what had just taken place. Probably not, we figured; it would be our word against his, and he would most likely deny the nature of the offer he made.

That's just what happened the next morning, when the parish secretary (back to work after a day's absence) called to inform me that "that NBC fellow is in with the pastor, and you better get over here, because Fr. Bulakowski's blood pressure is getting higher and higher, and he's not a well man." I went immediately to the rectory and joined their conversation. Now the NBC man was upset.

"The pastor here has been telling me that you called last night and told him I tried to blackmail you," he said, "when you know I would never try something like that." I responded by saying Fr. Bulakowski was given an accurate description of last night's meeting, including a precise report on what he, the producer, had said to me in the presence of a colleague. Given the content of that conversation, it was not surprising the pastor had reacted as strongly as he did, I argued. Fr. Bulakowski then began to object strenuously to the behavior of the film crew, both in Hamtramck and in the parish, and lectured the producer on the need for sensitivity toward ethnic groups. The pastor was articulate and forceful. While he was talking, the secretary showed in a young

Polish American who had been at the Hamtramck bar where the staged scene had been filmed. He entered the discussion and vigorously protested the manner in which a representative of a national network had approached a story on Polish Americans. Finally, Fr. Bulakowski and I reiterated our reasons for not having the community identified, and the stormy session ended. While the field producer said he could not guarantee that the film we objected to would not be shown on the national news, as of this writing, to our knowledge, it has never been aired.

A month had gone by since I presented that nine-page paper on a Sunday afternoon in Boston. In all, I received over two hundred letters and nearly as many phone calls. Perhaps 10 percent of those were positive. In addition, sixty-five scholars from a variety of disciplines wrote requesting copies of the paper. Many included lengthy letters expressing a keen interest in the subject matter, and some were struck by the similarity between my findings and their own research and personal experiences. In the following weeks Polish-American leaders from various cities contacted me to apologize for not getting in touch before they commented on inaccurate newspaper accounts. Locally, I spoke at numerous Polish-American gatherings and was given an opportunity to tell my side of the story. While many people remain hostile, most were understanding and cordial.

The parishioners of St. Thaddeus, with few exceptions, have always been supportive. Indeed, some of the families I interviewed for the study called and wished me luck. And several individuals, recognizing their quoted remarks in the newspaper accounts, remarked that reading them in print had provoked some interesting family discussions, even an argument or two, but that no harm was done. "You take good notes," said one woman, "and when we read in the paper what we had told you it was like holding up a mirror." Although these experiences which I have described were unpleasant, the parishioners of St. Thaddeus made them bearable. Always kind and gracious, they worried about me and my family, and casually dismissed the pain I had inadvertently caused them. Such an attitude was admirable, and I shall never forget them for it.

But, why all the publicity? First, according to some observers, the annual meeting of the AAAS attracts more media coverage than almost any other professional gathering in the United States. So I was in the right place at the right time (or, perhaps, the wrong place at the right time). Secondly, as the reporter with whom I shared a taxi pointed out, my paper was a "good story" because it was about real people, not abstract theories, and it was filled with "quotable quotes." Third, my attempt to convince a newspaper *(The Detroit Free Press)* not to print the story attracted the attention of other journalists attending the conference. After all, to correspondents searching for a story, there must have been something exciting in my paper, or I wouldn't have spent time attempting a "cover-up." Finally, in the late 1970s, ethnicity and blue-collar workers are "hot topics." I've spoken with numerous reporters, editors, and even journalism professors since February 1976, and they all support such an interpretation. Some pointed out that in cities with large Polish-American populations, like Detroit, Buffalo, Chicago, Rochester, and Philadelphia, a newspaper would be foolish not to print—and play up—a story dealing with that ethnic group. "It will sell papers," said an editorial writer for a New England newspaper, "and a publisher would be a damn fool not to take advantage of the situation."

Andrew Greeley feels there are other reasons the press publicized my findings so widely and interpreted them the way they did:

> They [Polish Americans] are the group most hated by the American intellectual and cultural elite. They are the ones most frequently stereotyped by the self-proclaimed liberals. They are the ones most despised by the "better people" in the country. They are the ones often patronized by American writers.

> The important part of the young sociologist's finding is that Polish blue-collar workers are making more money than the national average for their occupations. The press seized on the hard-work, self-sacrifice themes and exploited them for all they were worth. For there is nothing worse in American society, of course, than hard work and self-sacrifice. How old-fashioned, how dull, how self-rejecting, how Slavic.

> They used to call it the Protestant ethic, but now that it has gone out of fashion, they call it "the Slavic ethic."

The newspapers don't bother to note that hard work and self-sacrifice are the only methods by which a despised immigrant group can pull itself up by its own bootstraps and become successful in American society. And the Poles have done just that, despite the predictions of those who devised the immigration legislation of a half century ago that Poles simply could not become good (read successful) Americans.

The Poles have proven those bigots wrong. But they aren't getting credit for their success and they are patronized for their hard work and self-sacrifice.[10]

Greeley summarizes the role of the media in this affair, and also provides some insight into the reaction of Polish-American leaders in the following remarks:

The national media latched onto every tiny bit of it [the Boston paper] which fit the existing stereotype of the dumb, passive Poles and ignored the rest of his work. The Polish community leaders, understandably but unfortunately also characteristically, also shot from the hip without bothering to read the Wrobel report. Thus they gave the stereotype even more publicity.[11]

Greeley's analysis of how Polish leaders reacted to my paper brings me to another point. In general, Polish Americans responded in one of two ways to the local and national publicity. Some, by far the majority, believed I was calling members of this ethnic group unintelligent, stolid, and dull, and that I said there was something wrong with hard work and sacrifice.

These people were angry and wrote letters and made phone calls to speak out, to argue that they are intelligent, that hard work does bring success, such as children with master's degrees, a paid-off mortgage, a steady job, and a happy marriage. Writing in *Newsweek*, Michael Novak analyzed what had happened:

From many hundreds of hours of inquiry in one Polish-American neighborhood [Wrobel has shown] how deeply the public stereotype has been internalized by many Polish Americans. When a news dispatch carried his findings back to Detroit from the scholarly meeting in Boston where he presented them, the Detroit papers received a most touching deluge of letters from sad and hurt Polish Americans. Their own self-image was exactly as he described: poignantly aware of being stigmatized as dull, dumb, and stolid, and

> painfully aware of how unfair that image is, they could hardly bear
> to have the subject discussed. One cannot read these letters without
> piercing recognition and dismay.[12]

While that is true, people did vehemently object to how they were
being stigmatized by an unfavorable image. In a sense, then, while
individuals directed their anger and criticism at me, they were in
fact addressing the larger society.

Others reacted quite differently. They were more concerned
about "a limited and biased survey, an inadequate sample." But
more to the point, some Polish Americans, especially college
graduates and post–World War II immigrants, said I had studied
the "wrong" people. "You studied people who have no culture"
was the most common theme from those respondents. "Why not
study those of us who have an education, who work at white-collar
jobs? Then you would find out that we are an intelligent people,"
many said. Thus some Polish Americans share the same attitudes
as the larger society toward members of their own ethnic group
who are blue-collar workers.

Social scientists and representatives of the media need to be
aware of how cultural differences between the two groups inhibit
communication and often result in misunderstandings and inaccuracies that are passed on to the general public. Indeed, an anthropologist and a reporter meet as strangers, each carrying cultural
baggage from their respective work environments. The language of
social science is not always understood by journalists, and the time
constraints a reporter faces seem incomprehensible and unfair to
an anthropologist who is asked to summarize three years of work in
three minutes. Yet social scientists have a responsibility to communicate their findings to the general public. In analyzing why
that happens so infrequently, Brian Weiss places part of the blame
on academicians:

> Social scientists usually express hurt and amazement when their
> efforts and accomplishments come under public assault, particu-
> larly when the aggressor is a congressman or an unhappy taxpayer.
> Our task, we tell each other, is huge, diffuse, and complex, and
> those who criticize must lack the ability to see that complexity.
> What we don't say is that our own unwillingness to communicate
> has sown the seeds of public misunderstanding.[13]

He also advises:

> Compounding this problem [the fact that publication in academic journals is the usual method of gaining promotions] is the misapprehension on the part of many social scientists about what will happen to their data if they are exposed to the media. Just as a researcher takes care in the collection of his data, he can take care in its reporting. There exists an ever-expanding corps of people who have advanced training in the social sciences and experience as journalists, and these people wish to see their colleagues' research reported both accurately and intelligibly. By seeking out reporters and editors with the necessary training and experience, social scientists can not only protect themselves from inaccuracy, but also communicate more effectively to the public. [14]

Weiss is correct, but it is not always possible to "seek out reporters and editors with the necessary training and experience." Furthermore, the problem is exacerbated by those journalists who aggressively pursue a story with little regard for accuracy, and a flair for sensationalism. And while communication between social scientists and representatives of the news media could be better, that is only part of the problem. Publishers, editors, and journalists also need to become more sensitive toward ethnic groups.

What I have related so far did have an effect on how I revised my doctoral dissertation for publication. I tried to keep the jargon to a minimum and write for both social scientists and the general reader. I took greater care in choosing words that said what I meant, so my findings would be clear and not easily subject to misinterpretation. Toward that end I also elaborated on certain matters and included new research findings relevant to the subject being discussed. Yet the present manuscript does not differ substantially from the original in terms of how I perceived the way of life in one particular Polish-American community. And I am fully aware of the fact that another observer might have studied the same community and described things quite differently.

But, as Robert Redfield reminds us, "there is no one ultimate and utterly objective account of a human whole. Each account, if it preserves the human quality at all, is a created product in which the human qualities of the creator—the outside viewer and describer—are one ingredient." [15]

Notes

1: INTRODUCTION

1. My family and I lived in this community for four years and nine months. But the formal data-gathering phase of the study lasted only eighteen months, from October 1971 to June 1973. We left the community in July 1976.

2. Msgr. Geno Baroni, Unpublished Background Statement Prepared for a Workshop on Urban Ethnic Community Development, Co-sponsored by The United States Catholic Conference, Task Force on Urban Problems, and The Catholic University of America, Washington, D.C., June 15–18, 1970.

3. As quoted in Frye Gaillard, "Poles in Detroit Ally with Blacks," *Race Relations Reporter* 2 (1971): 9.

4. William I. Thomas and Florian Znaniecki, *The Polish Peasant in Europe and America* (New York: Dover Publications, 1958).

5. See, for example, Milton Gordon, *Assimilation in American Life* (New York: Oxford University Press, 1964); and Judith P. Kramer, *The American Minority Community* (New York: Thomas and Crowell, 1970). Also see Joseph Fichter, S.J., *Social Relations in the Urban Parish* (Chicago: University of Chicago Press, 1954); and John D. Donovan, "The Sociology of the Parish," *New Catholic Encyclopedia*, Vol. 10 (New York: McGraw-Hill, 1967), pp. 1019–20.

6. Our rented house badly needed a paint job and some minor repairs. When we moved in there was no lawn to speak of and the front sidewalk was cracked and in generally poor condition. After we had lived in the house for six months, several friends diplomatically suggested that we find "a nicer place to live." That was not surprising considering the excellent condition of most homes in the neighborhood, and the importance placed on "keeping up one's property."

7. Herbert Gans, *The Urban Villagers* (New York: The Free Press, 1962), p. 74.

8. Bennett Berger, *Working-Class Suburb: A Study of Auto Workers in Suburbia* (Berkeley: University of California Press, 1969). My interview schedule is available in the original study, "An Ethnographic Study of a Polish-American Parish and Neighborhood" (Ph.D. diss., Catholic University, 1975).

9. All the couples interviewed were Polish Americans. In sixteen of the twenty interviews both husband and wife were second-generation. Of the remaining four couples, two were of the third-generation, one was first, and in the last the husband was third and the wife was second.

173

10. The parish maintained a computerized listing of all parishioners who made regular financial contributions. Generally speaking, those individuals were heads of households.

11. Gans, *Urban Villagers*, pp. 330–39.

12. Ibid., p. 339.

13. Paul Wrobel, "Notes on 'Organizing' a Polish American Community," David W. Hartman, ed., "Immigrants and Migrants: The Detroit Ethnic Experience," special issue of the *Journal of University Studies* 10 (1974): 137–41.

2: ON METHODS, MOTIVES, AND MYTHS:
Past Research on Polish Americans

1. Robert Coles, "In Praise of Complexity, Ambiguity, Inconsistency, and Contrariness," *R F Illustrated* 3 (December 1976): 9.

2. Robert Redfield, "The Art of Social Science," *The American Journal of Sociology* 54 (1948): 188.

3. Ruth Tabrah, *Pulaski Place* (New York: Harper and Brothers, 1950); Millard Lampell, *The Hero* (New York: J. Messner, 1949).

4. Thomas and Znaniecki, *The Polish Peasant*; Neil C. Sandberg, *Ethnic Identity and Assimilation: The Polish American Community in Los Angeles* (New York: Praeger, 1974).

5. For the most complete review of the social science literature on Polish Americans, see Irwin T. Sanders and Ewa T. Morawska, *Polish American Community Life: A Survey of Research* (Boston: Boston University and the Polish Institute of Arts and Sciences in America, 1975).

6. Thomas and Znaniecki, *The Polish Peasant*.

7. Robert Bierstedt, ed., *The Making of Society: An Outline of Sociology* (New York: Random House, 1959), p. 419.

8. Alex Inkeles, *What Is Sociology?* (Englewood Cliffs, N.J.: Prentice-Hall, 1964), p. 51.

9. Herbert Blumer concludes his analysis of *The Polish Peasant* with a list of "some of the more important contributions which have made [the study] meritorious and which explain the profound influence which it has had on sociology and social psychology." His list includes:

1. A demonstration of the need of studying the subjective factor in social life.
2. The proposing of human documents as source material, particularly the life record, thus introducing what is known as the life history technique.
3. A statement of social theory which outlines the framework of a social psychology and the features of a sociology. The view of social psychology as the subjective aspect of culture has been particularly influential.
4. A statement of scientific method which has stimulated and reinforced the interest in making sociology a scientific discipline.
5. A number of important theories, such as that of personality, that of social control, that of disorganization, and that of the four wishes.
6. A variety of concepts which have gained wide acceptance, such as attitude, value, life organization, definition of situation, and the four wishes.
7. A rich content of insights, provocative generalizations, and shrewd observations.
8. An illuminating and telling characterization of the Polish peasant society.
   Herbert Blumer, *An Appraisal of Thomas and Znaniecki's The Polish Peasant*

in Europe and America (New York: Social Science Research Council, 1939), pp. 81–82.

And Janowitz has summarized this contribution in a discussion of W. I. Thomas and his work: "With the publication of *The Polish Peasant* he [Thomas] achieved a commanding intellectual position. It was a comprehensive study with a level of theoretical sophistication and empirical detail which had not yet been achieved. The richness he displayed in explaining the structures and mechanisms of social control and the explication of the personal responses—disruptive and integrative—meant that sociological analysis had been transformed." Morris Janowitz, ed., *W. I. Thomas on Social Disorganization and Social Personality* (Chicago: University of Chicago Press, 1966), p. lii.

10. Blumer, *Appraisal of The Polish Peasant*, p. 32.

11. Ibid., p. 75.

12. Thomas and Znaniecki, *The Polish Peasant*, pp. vii–viii.

13. Quoted in Blumer, *Appraisal of the Polish Peasant*, pp. 104–5.

14. Ibid., pp. 105–6.

15. Thomas and Znaniecki, *The Polish Peasant*, p. 1128.

16. Ibid., p. 1752.

17. Ibid., pp. 1751–52.

18. Theresita Polzin, *The Polish Americans: Whence and Whither* (Pulaski, Wis.: Franciscan Publishers, 1973); John L. Thomas, *The American Catholic Family* (Englewood Cliffs, N.J.: Prentice-Hall, 1956); Charles T. O'Reilly and Margaret M. Pembroke, *Older People in a Chicago Community* (Ann Arbor, Mich.: Braun-Brumfeld, 1957).

19. Quoted in Polzin, *Polish Americans*, p. 207.

20. Ibid., p. 210.

21. Ibid., p. 210. This is paradoxical in light of Thomas and Znaniecki's insightful observations on the social and religious functions of Polish parishes in the U.S. See pages 34–35, where I discuss those cogent impressions.

22. John L. Thomas, *American Catholic Family*.

23. Arthur Evans Wood, *Hamtramck Then and Now: A Sociological Study of a Polish-American Community* (New Haven: College and University Press, 1955).

24. Ibid., p. 45.

25. Ibid., p. 13.

26. Ibid., p. 27.

27. Ibid., p. 64.

28. Ibid., pp. 232–33.

29. Ibid., p. 234.

30. See, for example, Larry Wilde, *The Official Polish-Italian Joke Book* (New York: Pinnacle Books. 1973).

31. Niles Carpenter and Daniel Katz, "The Cultural Adjustment of the Polish Group in the City of Buffalo: An Experiment in the Technique of Social Investigation," *Social Forces* 6 (1927): 76–85.

32. Peter A. Ostafin, "The Polish Community in Transition: A Study of Group Interaction as a Function of Symbiosis and Common Definitions" (Ph.D. diss., University of Michigan, 1948).

33. Eugene E. Obidinski, "Ethnic to Status Group: A Study of Polish Americans in Buffalo" (Ph.D. diss., State University of New York at Buffalo, 1968).

34. Sandberg, *Ethnic Identity and Assimilation*.

35. Ibid., p. 4.

36. Ibid., p. 62.

37. Stanley Mackun, "The Changing Patterns of Polish Settlements in the Greater Detroit Area" (Ph.D. diss., University of Michigan, 1964).

38. Ibid., p. 89.

39. For a sociological overview of Polonia as a whole, see Helena Znaniecki Lopata, *Polish Americans: Status Competition in an Ethnic Community* (Englewood Cliffs, N.J.: Prentice-Hall, 1976).

40. Robert K. Yin, ed., *Race, Creed, Color, or National Origin: A Reader on Racial and Ethnic Identities in American Society* (Itasca, Ill.: F. E. Peacock, 1973).

41. Quoted in Milton M. Gordon, *Assimilation in American Life*, p. 120.

42. Milton M. Gordon, "Assimilation in America: Theory and Reality," in Yin, *Race, Creed, Color*, pp. 34–44.

43. Ibid., p. 42.

44. Gordon, *Assimilation in American Life*, p. 113.

45. Yin, *Race, Creed, Color*, p. xiii.

46. Bennett Berger, "Suburbia and the American Dream," in Yin, *Race, Creed, Color*, p. 113.

47. Ibid., p. 112.

48. Gordon, *Assimilation in American Life*, pp. 130–31.

49. Ruby Jo Reeves Kennedy, "Single or Triple Melting-Pot? Intermarriage Trends in New Haven," *American Journal of Sociology* 49 (1944): 331–39; Will Herberg, *Protestant, Catholic, Jew* (Garden City, N.Y.: Anchor Books, 1960).

50. Nathan Glazer and Daniel Patrick Moynihan, *Beyond the Melting Pot* (Cambridge, Mass.: M.I.T. Press, 1963), p. 17.

51. Harold J. Abramson, *Ethnic Diversity in Catholic America* (New York: John Wiley & Sons, 1973), p. 179.

3: THE SETTING

1. Robert Sinclair, *The Face of Detroit* (Detroit: Department of Geography, Wayne State University, 1972), p. 10.

2. Ibid., p. 9.

3. Ibid.

4. Frank Angelo, "Detroit's Ethnicity: An Historical Perspective," in Malvina Hauk Abonyi et al., eds., *Ethni-City: A Guide to Ethnic Detroit* (Detroit: Michigan Ethnic Heritage Studies Center and Ethnic Studies Division, Wayne State University, 1976), p. 13.

5. Mackun, "Changing Patterns of Polish Settlements," p. 68.

6. Ibid., p. 69.

7. Ibid., p. 65.

8. Lois Rankin, "Detroit Nationality Groups," *Michigan History Magazine* 22 (1939): 134.

9. U.S. Bureau of the Census, *U.S. Census of Population and Housing: 1960*, Michigan, Final Report PHC(1)40 (Washington, D.C.: Government Printing Office, 1962); U.S. Bureau of the Census, *U.S. Census of Population and*

Housing: 1970, Michigan, Final Report PHC(1)5B (Washington, D.C.: Government Printing Office, 1972). The demographic data in the following paragraph are also from these two sources.

10. The most recent estimates are that between 1974 and 1975 Detroit lost 20,400 residents. This represents an 11.9 percent drop in total population since 1970. Although precise figures are unavailable, Detroit's Black population is now (1977) estimated at between 52 and 60 percent of the total.

11. U.S. Bureau of the Census, *U.S. Census of Population:* 1970, Vol. 1, *Characteristics of the Population. Part 24, Michigan.* (Washington, D.C.: Government Printing Office, 1973).

12. Malvina Hauk Abonyi, et al., *Ethnic-City.*

13. Unless otherwise noted, the information on St. Albertus is from the following source: Rev. Joseph Swastek, *Detroit's Oldest Polish Parish: St. Albertus* (Detroit: St. Albertus Parish, 1973).

14. One author argues that the early Polish settlers had an additional reason for wanting their own parish: they were rebuffed in their attempts to participate in the German community. Here is how Radzialowski summarized the situation: "The Poles offered to join the German community in financing and building the new church of St. Joseph. After some deliberation the Germans agreed, on the condition that the Poles sit in special pews separate from the rest of the congregation. Enraged, the Poles withdrew and organized their own parish, St. Albertus, which was to be larger and more magnificent than the new German church." Thaddeus C. Radzialowski, "A View from the Polish Ghetto," *Ethnicity* 1 (1974): 127.

15. There are conflicting theories as to why Bishop Borgess was reluctant to give immediate approval to the formation of a Polish parish. While the official history of St. Albertus mentions his financial concerns, Radzialowski suggests that the bishop was less than fond of Poles or "Polishness," and that he later made several decisions which threatened the existence of the Polish community. Implicit in Radzialowski's remarks, then, is the notion that Bishop Borgess was deeply prejudiced against the Poles and thus hesitant to permit the establishment of a Polish parish. Cf. Swastek, *Detroit's Oldest Parish* and Radzialowski, "Polish Ghetto." For an in-depth account of Detroit's early Polish parishes and their often stormy relationship with the chancery, see Ostafin, "Polish Community in Transition."

16. Thomas and Znaniecki, *The Polish Peasant,* pp. 41–42.

17. Mackun, "Changing Patterns of Polish Settlement," p. 36.

18. Most Roman Catholic parishes in the United States are territorial: their parishioners are individuals who reside within specific geographic boundaries. National parishes are quite different. They were established by the church to meet the special needs of Catholic immigrant groups and are based on membership in an ethnic group rather than residence in a given locality.

19. C. J. Nuesse and Thomas J. Harte, C.SS.R., eds., *The Sociology of the Parish* (Milwaukee: Bruce Publishing Company, 1951), p. 5.

20. Thomas and Znaniecki, *The Polish Peasant,* p. 42.

21. This figure is based on a computerized listing of all contributors. The parish maintains this listing to facilitate the mailing of envelopes in which contributions are made.

22. John D. Donovan, "The Social Structure of the Parish," in Nuesse and Harte, *Sociology of the Parish,* p. 87.

23. Ibid., p. 90.

24. Ibid., p. 92.

25. I have chosen the term "network" to describe the informal structure of the parish because not all families have social relationships with one another, as in an organized group. This usage is in accord with the work of John Barnes, who defines a network as follows: "Each person is, as it were, in touch with a number of people, some of whom are directly in touch with each other and some of whom are not. . . . " Quoted in Elizabeth Bott, *Family and Social Network* (London: Tavistock Publications, 1957), p. 59.

26. The 1970 R. L. Polk Directory for Detroit listed 1,199 housing units in the area studied. Each listing included both an address and the names of an individual. Of those 1,199 names and addresses, 863, or 72 percent, belonged to St. Thaddeus according to parish records for 1972.

27. In this context the term "parishioner" refers to those individuals, both married and single, who regularly contribute to the financial support of St. Thaddeus through the use of envelopes provided by the parish. In April of 1972 there were 1,218 such individuals, most of whom are the heads of households. Since the parish maintains a computerized listing of these parishioners (for mailing purposes) it was a relatively simple task to plot their distribution on a larger map provided by the Planning Department of the City of Detroit. Of the 1,218 individuals listed, 863, or 71 percent, lived in the geographic area surrounding the parish.

28. Suzanne Keller, *The Urban Neighborhood: A Sociological Perspective* (New York: Random House, 1968), p. 156.

29. For a review of how the concept of community has been used in the social sciences, see George A. Hillery, "Definitions of Community: Areas of Agreement," *Rural Sociology* 20 (1955): 111–23.

30. Roland L. Warren, *The American Community* (Chicago: Rand McNally, 1964), pp. 9–10.

31. Ibid., p. 27.

32. Ibid., pp. 174–75.

33. Ibid., p. 177.

34. Judith Blake and Kingsley Davis, "On Norms and Values," in Robert A. Manners and David Kaplan, eds., *Theory in Anthropology* (Chicago: Aldine Publishing Company, 1968), p. 469.

35. S. F. Nadel, "Social Control and Self Regulation," *Social Forces* 31 (1953): 270. Following Radcliffe-Brown's definition, organized social sanctions "are social action carried out according to some traditional and recognized procedure," while diffuse or unorganized sanctions, like gossip and ridicule, "are spontaneous expressions of approval or disapproval by members of the community acting as individuals." A. R. Radcliffe-Brown, "Social Sanctions," *Encyclopedia of the Social Sciences*, Vol. 13 (New York: Macmillan, 1934), p. 533.

36. John Thomas, *American Catholic Family*.

37. Warren, *American Community*.

38. Ibid., p. 96.

39. Raymond Breton, "Institutional Completeness of Ethnic Communities and the Personal Relations of Immigrants," *American Journal of Sociology* 70 (1964): 193–205.

40. Conrad M. Arensberg and Solon T. Kimball, *Culture and Community* (New York: Harcourt, Brace and World, 1965), p. 99.

41. The data reported in this and the following paragraphs are from the 1970 U.S. Census. U.S. Bureau of the Census, *Census of Population and Housing:* 1970.

4: THE FAMILY

1. Bott, *Family and Social Network.*

2. Alexander Rysman, "How the 'Gossip' Became a Woman," *Journal of Communication* 27 (1977): 176.

3. Sally Yerkovich, "Gossiping as a Way of Speaking," *Journal of Communication* 27 (1977): 192.

4. Gossip also serves as the medium through which individuals establish, maintain, or lose social status and rank. But I disagree with Helena Znaniecki Lopata, who argues that status competition is the most distinguishing characteristic of Polish-American community life. See Helena Znaniecki Lopata, *Polish Americans: Status Competition.* For my review of her book, see *Polish American Studies* 33 (1976): 65–68.

5. One sociologist has termed such friends "confidants." See Mirra Komarovsky, *Blue-Collar Marriage* (New York: Vintage Books, 1967), p. 207.

6. Lillian Breslow Rubin, *Worlds of Pain: Life in the Working-Class Family* (New York: Basic Books, 1976), p. 21.

7. Ibid., p. 221.

8. Peter H. Mann, "The Concept of Neighborliness," *American Journal of Sociology* 60 (1954): 163–68.

9. That phrase was used as a chapter title to describe neighboring in a community studied by Michael Young and Peter Willmott, in *Family and Kinship in East London* (London: Routledge and Kegan Paul, 1957).

10. See, for example, Floyd Dotson, "Patterns of Voluntary Association among Urban Working-Class Families," *American Sociological Review* 26 (1961): 687–93; Eugene Litwak, "Geographic Mobility and Extended Family Cohesion," *American Sociological Review* 25 (1965): 385–94; and Marc Fried, *The World of the Urban Working Class* (Cambridge, Mass.: Harvard University Press, 1973).

11. Fried, *Urban Working Class,* p. 106.

12. Roughly 20 percent of all families have relatives who reside in the neighborhood.

13. Recent immigrants socialize primarily with relatives. Also, the community is slow to accept newcomers, even those who speak Polish. Further, the new immigrants feel uncomfortable in a setting where English is the first language. They view Polish-American residents as "cold" and "unfriendly." One man, who arrived here from Poland only five years ago, observed: "In Poland everybody is friendly; they greet you as you walk past their homes and even invite you in for a drink. But here people keep to themselves. They don't seem interested in getting to know me." Thus what we have referred to as "latent neighborliness" is a characteristic which appears to be uncommon in Poland.

14. The phrase is Irving M. Levine's, director of the America Jewish Committee's Institute on Pluralism and Group Identity. He defines economic trauma as

"the mental state that accompanies economic uncertainty; it is a more accurate statement of the current national condition than the fact of unemployment alone. Economic trauma means the fear of unemployment as well as unemployment itself. . . . Economic trauma triggers stress and worry about such things as job availability as well as job security, bills, taxes, and the record high cost of food and other essential commodities." From unpublished statement prepared for a consultation entitled "The Human Costs of Economic Trauma: Impact on Children and Families," co-sponsored by the Institute on Pluralism and Group Identity and the Merrill-Palmer Institute, Detroit, Michigan, June 21, 1976.

15. Rubin, *Worlds of Pain*, p. 94.

16. Ibid.

17. The fact that most couples in this community approve of divorce in principle is a surprising finding in light of Obidinski's data on this question from a study of Polish Americans in Buffalo, New York. He reports that two-thirds of his respondents—from both the second and third generation—disapprove of divorce. Obidinski, *Ethnic to Status Group*, p. 73.

18. Gans, *Urban Villagers*, p. 51.

19. Ibid., p. 52.

20. Rubin, *Worlds of Pain*; Komarovsky, *Blue-Collar Marriage*; and Fried, *Urban Working Class*.

21. According to U.S. Census data, 39.2 percent of all women sixteen and over in this neighborhood were employed in 1970. But only 23 percent of the married women (with husbands present) were working during that same year. U.S. Bureau of the Census, *Census of Population and Housing:* 1970. In the current study, out of twenty married women interviewed, only four or 20 percent were employed.

22. Rubin, *Worlds of Pain*, p. 96.

23. While this chapter tends to focus on the relationship between boys and their parents, especially the father, the patterns of child-rearing discussed are essentially the same for males and females. But there is one major difference: Parents consider it less important for young women to attend college. As one father said, "Girls just get married and have kids, so all that learning is a waste of time and money." That does not mean, however, that girls are allowed to be less obedient or self-disciplined than the boys.

24. For an excellent analysis of attitudes toward blue-collar workers, see Patricia Cayo Sexton and Brendan Sexton, *Blue Collars and Hard Hats* (New York: Random House, 1971). They write, for example, "The image of the blue-collar worker, as reflected in the media, is as distorted, and in some respects as debased and vicious, as Hitler's stereotypes of the Jews" (p. 73).

25. As part of a provocative study on working-class consciousness in Detroit, John C. Leggett asked members from various groups to " rate their chances to be accepted into a white middle-class country club." He reported that "the percentages . . . and the mean rank scores agree on an order of group prestige ranging from highest to lowest in status: the English, Germans, Poles, and Negroes, respectively. Their own group membership notwithstanding, raters agreed on this ethnic hierarchy. For example, the majority of Poles, Negroes, Germans and English ranked Poles in the third position." Leggett's findings are strong evidence of the low status of Polish Americans, and the fact that they are aware of their social standing. See John C. Leggett, *Class, Race, and Labor* (London: Oxford University Press, 1968), p. 109.

26. Richard Sennett and Jonathan Cobb, *The Hidden Injuries of Class* (New York: Vintage Books, 1972).

27. Ibid., p. 164.

28. Ibid., p. 128.

29. On the basis of survey research data gathered by the National Opinion Research Center, William McCready has argued that Polish-American males and females "find the mother less salient in their lives than the father." "The Persistence of Ethnic Variation in American Families," Andrew M. Greeley, ed., *Ethnicity in the United States: A Preliminary Reconnaissance* (New York: John Wiley & Sons, 1974), p. 168. My interviews and observations suggest just the opposite, especially with regard to the relationship between males and their fathers. For when a son hears his father say "Don't be like me," he may begin to wonder if his father is a failure, a person who was unable to rise above the very work he so despises. And when this happens, the son might turn to his mother for emotional support and advice, feeling that she is the stronger of the two parents. Furthermore, I have already discussed how women have attained status and power within the family. So I would argue that it is the mother who is more salient for both boys and girls in a Polish-American working-class family.

30. Tabrah, *Pulaski Place*, pp. 118–19.

31. Gans, *Urban Villagers*, p. 59.

32. M. L. Kohn, *Class and Conformity: A Study of Values* (Homewood, Ill.: Dorsey Press, 1969); Rubin, *Worlds of Pain;* Urie Bronfenbrenner, "Socialization and Social Class Through Time and Space," in Reinhardt Bendix and Seymour M. Lipset, eds., *Class, Status, and Power* (New York: Free Press, 1966), pp. 362–77.

33. Robert A. LeVine, "Parental Goals: A Cross Cultural View," in Hope Jensen Leichter, ed., *The Family as Educator* (New York: Teachers College Press, 1974), p. 63.

34. Ibid.

35. Ibid., pp. 63–64.

36. For a more detailed examination of this matter, see Wrobel, "Notes on 'Organizing'," in Hartman, "Immigrants and Migrants."

37. These remarks on the problems of Polish-American children who go on to college or white-collar jobs are based on direct observation as well as conversations with college professors and employers. For example, one professor from Wayne State University told me he could always "pick out" his Polish-American students: They were conscientious, bright, but shy and very reluctant when it came to participating in classroom discussions.

38. Richard Gambino has written about some of the difficulties faced by young Italian Americans who leave the security of their ethnic families for the larger society: "Although he [the young Italian American] usually is diligent and highly responsible, the other elements needed for a powerful personality are paralyzed by his pervasive identity crisis. His ability for sustained action with autonomy, initiative, self-confidence, and assertiveness is undermined by his yearning for ego integrity." "La Famiglia: Four Generations of Italian-Americans," in Joseph A. Ryan, ed., *White Ethnics: Life in Working-Class America* (Englewood Cliffs, N.J.: Prentice-Hall, 1973), p. 51.

39. In 1970, nearly 75 percent of all young adults aged twenty and twenty-one

were not enrolled in school. Further, 21 percent of those between the ages of sixteen and twenty-one had not graduated from high school. U.S. Bureau of the Census, *Census of Population and Housing:* 1970.

40. While scholarships and other forms of financial aid are made available to Blacks, Chicanos, and other minority groups, American society has yet to recognize the very real economic needs of working-class Polish Americans, Italian Americans, and other national origin groups from Southern and Eastern Europe. Richard Krickus has most recently addressed this problem in *Pursuing the American Dream: White Ethnics and the New Populism* (Garden City, N.Y.: Anchor Books, 1976).

41. "Six American Families" was produced by Group W in association with the United Church of Christ and the United Methodist Church. It was shown on the Public Broadcasting System beginning April 4, 1977. The originating station was KQED, San Francisco, California.

42. For a fuller discussion of this matter, see Paul Wrobel, "The Polish American Experience: An Anthropological View of Ruth Tabrah's *Pulaski Place* and Millard Lampell's *The Hero*," [in press].

43. Sennett and Cobb, *Hidden Injuries of Class*, p. 31.

44. Ibid., p. 125.

5: THE PARISH

1. Raymond Breton, "Institutional Completeness of Ethnic Communities."

2. The figure reported here on the total number of parishioners for the year 1925 is from an album commemorating St. Thaddeus's fortieth anniversary, published in 1965. Figures for the years 1940, 1948, and 1954 are from canonical visitation reports obtained from archdiocesan archives.

3. At present this issue revolves around the archdiocesan assessment system. Under this system, or tax, as it is usually called, each parish is required to contribute a portion of its income (4 percent of the first $25,000, and 6 percent thereafter) to the archdiocesan treasury. The people of St. Thaddeus are angry because the money they earn from sponsoring an annual festival to keep their school open is considered parish income and thus subject to that tax. Further, since the archdiocese has supported Black inner-city parishes from their central fund (to the tune of $450,000 in 1975, for example), members of St. Thaddeus say, "Cardinal Dearden takes our hard-earned money and gives it to the Blacks. Yet he knows that to close our schools is to destroy our communities." Polish Americans also argue that money collected from the Archdiocesan Development Fund and the Inter-Parish Sharing Program is distributed to Black parishes, while their own are also struggling to survive. For more information on the relationship between Polish Americans in Detroit and the archdiocese, see Kazimierz Olejarczyk, "Ethnic Issues in the Church, "in Otto Feinstein, ed., *Ethnic Groups in the City* (Lexington, Mass.: D. C. Heath and Company, 1971), pp. 225–30. Also worthwhile is Marco Trbovich's "Angry Poles Say Liberalized Church Ignored Ethnics," *The Detroit Free Press*, March 28, 1973. For more general information on John Cardinal Dearden and the archdiocese, see Thomas C. Fox, "Cardinal Dearden an Enigma to Many," *The Detroit Free Press*, October 6, 1975; and, by the same author, two other articles: "Some Oppose Church Wealth," *The Detroit*

Free Press, October 8, 1975; and "School Crisis Grips Church," *The Detroit Free Press*, October 10, 1975.

4. When the adults in St. Thaddeus were children, purgatory was often spoken of by nuns and priests as though it were literally a *place*. The souls "who weren't quite ready for heaven" went to purgatory, and the only way to "get them out" was to pray. So parishioners often prayed for "the poor souls in purgatory," especially their loved ones.

5. Postponing first confession until after First Holy Communion was an experiment later terminated in a joint declaration from the Congregation of the Sacraments and of the Clergy, dated July 9, 1973. More recently, however, it has become common practice in some parishes.

6. The title of this program was "The Church, World, and Kingdom." It was designed by the archdiocese based on suggestions and recommendations from Synod/69, a convention of lay Catholics and clergy from Detroit who attempted to set guidelines for the church in this particular archdiocese. For a report on that gathering, see *Synod/69* (Detroit: Archdiocese of Detroit, 1969).

7. Clifford Geertz, *The Interpretation of Cultures* (New York: Basic Books, 1973), p. 89.

8. As quoted in Abramson, *Ethnic Diversity*, p. 126.

9. Ibid., p. 130.

10. Nearly 450 parishioners, both children and adults, belong to fifteen parish organizations. Without knowing the precise number of total parishioners it is impossible to state this figure accurately in terms of a percentage. But we would not be too far off base by suggesting that slightly less than 10 percent are actively involved in parish associations.

11. For an interesting description of the polka and its relevance as a subject worthy of further study, see Charles Keil, "How Did You Get Interested in the Polka Anyway?" *Ethos* 26 (1975): 19–20.

12. Rubin, *Worlds of Pain*, p. 127.

13. *Newsweek*, November 1, 1976, p. 81

14. "Back to Basics Is a Big Hit," *The Detroit Free Press*, October 11, 1976.

15. Ibid.

16. Jim Bishop, "The Nuns Were Hell-Bent on Making Us Kids Learn," *The Detroit Free Press*, April 10, 1976.

6: THE NEIGHBORHOOD

1. Statistics on crime in this census tract before 1966 are unavailable. But during that year 120 crimes were committed. In 1973 that figure rose to 265. There were only 6 armed robberies and 21 burglaries during 1966; seven years later those numbers increased to 18 and 46, respectively. Unfortunately, it is not possible to draw other comparisons between the two years because of differences in reporting and categorizing crimes. But 1973 statistics do provide information on what crimes were committed most often during that year. They, along with their frequency of occurrence, are as follows:

Breaking and Entering a Dwelling	46
Stolen Cars	37
Malicious Destruction of Property	33

Larceny   33
Armed Robbery   18

The figures included here are from official but unpublished reports of the Detroit Police Department on crimes committed by census tract for 1966 and 1973.

2. Andrew Greeley, "Ethnicity and Racial Attitudes: The Case of the Jews and Poles," *Ethnicity* 80 (1975): 929.

3. For a very interesting discussion of the relationship between crime and unemployment in Detroit, see Robert Conot, *American Odyssey* (New York: Bantam Books, 1975).

4. Andrew Hacker, "Getting Used to Mugging," *New York Review of Books* 20 (1973): 9.

5. Krickus, *Pursuing the American Dream*, pp. 386-87.

6. *The Detroit Free Press*, January 28, 1975.

7. For more information on "steering" in the Detroit area, see Howard Kohn, "15 Realty Firms Accused of Blockbusting," *The Detroit News*, August 17, 1972.

8. Ibid. A detailed discussion of this problem will also be found in Michael Maidenberg, "Outcry Mounts on Blockbusting," *The Detroit Free Press*, September 17, 1972.

9. Quoted in Maidenberg, "Outcry Mounts."

10. Carl Konzelman, "City's Values Rising, Not Declining," *The Detroit News*, November 21, 1971.

11. Ironically, what real estate salesmen say may be true, but only in the beginning. As McEntire points out, "House prices weaken in areas anticipating a racial change and many continue depressed during the early stages of transition, but after transition, prices rise again." Davis McEntire, "The Housing Market in Racially Mixed Areas," in Sandor Halebsky, ed., *The Sociology of the City* (New York: Charles Scribner's Sons, 1973), p. 187.

12. It is not unusual for a potential buyer to wait months before learning whether his mortgage application has been approved. Another separate but related factor is "red-lining," a lending institution's refusal to make loans in geographic areas they consider risks. While I did not investigate the extent to which that practice affects the St. Thaddeus neighborhood, several new residents did explain that banks and savings institutions were reluctant to lend them money for the purchase of a home in this section of the city.

13. U.S. Bureau of the Census, *Census of Population and Housing*: 1970.

14. For purposes of statistical analysis, Detroit has been divided into forty-nine sub-communities, geographic areas made up of several census tracts. The boundaries of those sub-communities were drawn by The City Planning Department and United Community Services, an organization concerned with the delivery of social services to neighborhood residents. The data reported here are drawn from *A Profile of Detroit: 1969* (Detroit: The Mayor's Committee for Community Renewal, 1970).

15. U.S. Bureau of the Census, *Census of Population and Housing*: 1960; U.S. Bureau of the Census, Census of Population and Housing: 1970.

16. Ibid.

17. Don Ball, a *Detroit News* reporter, has chronicled the scandalous mismanagement of HUD projects in Detroit, including the role of FHA's home mortgage programs, in a series of articles published during 1971 and 1972. They are an

important source for anyone attempting to understand the extent to which federal programs affect Detroit's neighborhoods.

18. Michael Novak, "Black and White in Catholic Eyes," *The New York Times Magazine*, November 16, 1975, p. 114.

19. An appropriate title for a book dealing with ethnicity and inter-ethnic relations. See Andrew Greeley, *Why Can't They Be Like Us?* (New York: The American Jewish Committee, 1969).

20. I personally counted all the "for sale" signs in this census tract on a block-by-block basis. According to U.S. Census data, the homes being sold represent slightly more than 4 percent of the total. U.S. Bureau of the Census, *Census of Population and Housing:* 1970.

21. Peter L. Berger and Richard John Neuhaus, *To Empower People: The Role of Mediating Structures in Public Policy* (Washington, D.C.: American Enterprise Institute for Public Policy Research, 1977), p. 8.

22. Ibid., p. 2.

23. Howard W. Hallman, *Neighborhood Government in a Metropolitan Setting* (Beverly Hills, Calif.: Sage Publications, 1974); Milton Kotler, *Neighborhood Government* (Indianapolis: Bobbs-Merrill, 1969).

24. Arthur J. Naparstek, *Policy Options for Neighborhood Empowerment* (Washington, D.C.: The Academy for Contemporary Problems, 1976).

25. As quoted in a newsletter published by the National Center for Urban Ethnic Affairs, Washington, D.C., January, 1977, p. 6.

26. Robert Reinhold, "A Priest is Stirring the Melting Pot to Revitalize Ethnic Neighborhoods," *The New York Times*, April 20, 1977.

27. Berger and Neuhaus, *To Empower People*, p. 8.

28. Richard Krickus and Stephen Adubato, "Stabilizing White Ethnic Neighborhoods," in Ryan, *White Ethnics*, p. 93.

7: CONCLUSION

1. Thomas and Znaniecki, *The Polish Peasant*.

2. Sandberg, *Ethnic Identity and Assimilation*.

3. Israel Zangwill, *The Melting Pot* (New York: Macmillan, 1909).

4. Sennett and Cobb, *Hidden Injuries of Class*, p. 128.

5. Berger and Neuhaus, *To Empower People*, p. 2.

6. Elliot Liebow, *Tally's Corner* (Boston: Little, Brown and Co., 1967), pp. 224–25.

7. Gordon, *Assimilation in American Life*, p. 253.

8: Ibid., p. 247.

9. Gans, *Urban Villagers*.

10. Rubin, *Worlds of Pain*.

EPILOGUE

1. Sennett and Cobb, *Hidden Injuries of Class*.

2. "Polish Americans," *Parade*, December 7, 1975.

3. Thomas O'Toole, "The Polish Stereotype," *The Washington Post*, February 23, 1976.

4. "Detroit Poles Feel They're Unworthy, Study Discloses," *The Detroit News*, February 23, 1976.

5. Dolores Katz, "Study Finds Bad Polish Image," *The Detroit Free Press*, February 23, 1976.

6. Ibid.

7. *The Detroit News*, February 24, 1976.

8. Mary Dedinsky, "Ethnic Study Stirs Strong Reaction, " *The Chicago Sun-Times*, February 25, 1976; "Ethnic Self-Image: No Joke," *The Chicago Sun-Times*, February 28, 1976.

9. "Wrobel Explains Survey on Poles," *The Detroit News*, February 28, 1976; "The Purpose of the Polish American Study," *The Detroit Free Press*, February 28, 1976.

10. Andrew Greeley, "In Defense of Polish Pride," *The Chicago Tribune*, March 9, 1976.

11. In connection with Greeley's remarks, it is interesting to note that a recently published sociological study of working-class families included the following comment on adult males: "After a lifetime of repressing his feelings, he often *is* a blank, unaware that he's thinking or feeling anything." Rubin, *Worlds of Pain*, p. 124. That is a very critical and perhaps unjustified conclusion. Yet there was no reaction from the media, even though the book has been widely discussed.

12. Michael Novak, "The Sting of Polish Jokes," *Newsweek*, April 12, 1976.

13. Brian Weiss, "Speaking of Social Science," *Human Organization* 35 (1976): 397.

14. Ibid., p. 398.

15. Robert Redfield, *The Little Community* and *Peasant Society and Culture* (a combined edition of two separate volumes) (Chicago: University of Chicago Press, 1969), p. 136.

Index